How I Faithed It Over

How I Faithed It Over

"Do You Trust God, or Don't You?"

Sonya M. Sessoms

SMS MINISTRIES

CONTENTS

CONTENTS

Published by SMS Ministries in Killeen, Texas. First Printing, 2020

Edited by Michelle L. Massie Early for ProEditor at www.proeditor.us.

SMS Ministries books may be purchased in bulk for educational, business, fundraising, or sales promotional use. For information about purchases/services, please email publishing@SMSMinistries.co.

Library of Congress Control Number: 2020909532

ISBN: 978-1-7350847-0-1

Dedicated To...

Juan aka Husband, Vidal, and Reid
I love you guys, and I pray I make you as proud of me as I
am of you. #FamilyFirst #SessomsFam #ThankYou

"My Lady" aka "Mom" aka Felicia Joye
You believed I could, so I did. I love you. #ThankYou

My late "Uncle Daddy" Victor Samuel Reid
To say that I miss you would not be an accurate assessment of my feelings after
losing you. You were everything to me, and you believed I could do it all. I've said
it before and will repeat it, "Thank you!" I will always love you.

My late grandparents,
Pop-Pop Noah and Grandma Carolyn Reid, II
Your level of encouragement and belief in me when I had no idea where to begin
this journey will stay in my heart. I finally stopped running...I'm walking in it
now. Thank you for paving the way.

My late grandmom and father,
Sarah Reid and Stanley Henderson
Although you left this earth before I could get to know you, thank you for
your prayers, love, and support while you were here. They were not in vain.

My late friend/brother Joseph H.M. Dawkins
Thank you for being a trailblazer in our lives. Thank you for being a
Freedom Fighter. You were loved. I miss you.

Reviews

"This book is so engaging as Sonya gives you an all-access pass into her life and her journey of faith. She teaches that you do not have to have a perfect life to develop an amazing faith. She shows us how it is in the imperfections of our lives, if we are spiritually awake, that we grow."
Dr. Larry L. Anderson Jr., Pastor, Great Commission Church, and Co-Author of *Ask Me Why I'm not in Church*

"Faith takes us "to" and "through." A life pleasing to God is based on faith. Often, we do not understand our journey and the details can baffle us as they unfold, all during the time of having to go to, and through, the "next." In her book *How I Faithed It Over,* Pastor Sonya Sessoms takes us through her experience in a life of F-A-I-T-H and offers a recipe for success. With those ingredients, this book turns out to be a wonderful DISH...**D**-elightful **I**-nsightful **S**-piritual **H**-elpful." **Keith I. Pelzer**, Pastor, Southern Baptist Church (Philadelphia, PA)

"This book holds in it an intimate reading journey of a life of faith growing internally. It invites warmly a moment of reflective interest that explains a personal development of faith with memories and challenges! The impactful summation statement is, "Faith is about Living!" An invitation was in order at the end. Thank you, Sonya, for sharing real living challenges!"
Dr. Paul R. Lee, Senior Pastor/Teacher, Jones Memorial Baptist Church

"Faith-inspiring, riveting, encouraging, motivating, and biblically informative, this book from author Pastor Sonya Sessoms takes us on a journey of faith as she shares her personal experiences while transitioning in life. There is a melodious flow of heartfelt sincerity and commitment that will be generated through each chapter to challenge the reader's faith. This book will truly motivate and prepare the readers from young students to adults, no matter what they encounter or whatever obstacles they may face, to never give up. As you walk into your destiny...continue to have faith in the Lord!"
Patricia A. Phillips, D.D., Apostle/Pastor/Founder, Nothing but the Word Deliverance Church

Thanks, and All of That

I am grateful for my *Mother*, who always told me that I was the best, even in my failures. She never allowed me to give up and made me try at least once before quitting. She laid a strong foundation in me of knowing and loving the Lord. She is a pillar in my life, and I am forever indebted to her for the sacrifices she's made to ensure my success always. To *Ma B and the late Papa John*, my in-loves, thank you so much. Papa John, you are missed and I was always blessed by how you loved me as if I were your own flesh and blood. Ma B thanks for being awesome! Thanks for giving this only child siblings too!

To my *TRIBE*...I'm glad that God gave me a group of individuals who just "get" me. Blood couldn't make us any tighter. I didn't want to name everyone, because I know I'd miss a couple, but thank you! I appreciate you all for being consistent and keeping me on my toes. And to the newest member, welcome, and thanks so much for not letting me lose sight of the goal! Each of y'all are the real MVPs. You know who you are. Hugz and Kissz!!!

To *Shellz mi Bellz aka Michelle*, THANK YOU for being my day oner. I tell you all the time that if you hadn't checked me and darn near forced me to live right, it would've taken me a lot longer to get to this place. You will ALWAYS be my sister from another mother and mister. You have helped me find myself and allowed me to find my voice, even during chaotic moments. You did this with no judgment. You are the quiet, but STRONG source of knowledge, love, and care that every woman needs in their lives. I'm thankful for the honor to call you family. My brother *Big Mike*, my *Knees*, and my *Twin* are my loves as well. I can only hope I'm there for you too.

To my Sissy, *Dr. Christal*...well...you know how it is. We went from me donating money to buy turkeys in church, to us being tighter than tight. We love hard and fight for one another even harder. We have both endured times of tumultuousity (my new word), but God kept us. Keep shining your light, give my nephew a pound, and bless you and your new husband. God is so amazing! Love you much.

I would be crazy not to thank one of my favorite professors-turned-big-brother, **Dr. LA**, and the man who was responsible for pushing me to go to seminary, **Dr. Walls**. You two gentlemen made a significant impact on my growth, and although we are not all sitting up and hanging out anymore, because of life and its many changes, you guys (and your wives and children) are my family until the end. I will always keep the genuine love you have for my family and me tucked in my heart pocket. I heart y'all for real. I miss y'all in TX, Dr. Walls. We had some dope times!!!

To **NissBiss, aka Aronissa**, you're a rare one. You single-handedly took residence in my life when I needed a big sister. In my eyes, you could do no wrong. I love you. Our life is a book in and of itself, so I will simply say LS, HTG...LOL! Don't forget to squeeze your hubby, **Marvin** and my **DaniPooh**. To **Bobert**, thanks for loving me like your sister and giving me another family. You stepped right in and looked out for the kids and me when your brother was serving the country. I will always love you for your sincerity and your heart of pure mushiness. Kiss your beautiful wife, **Larissa** for me and squeeze **Kiara** and **CiCi**. You ROCK!

If I didn't say thank you to my original **1Prayz** family, I'd just be an idiot...you all were my first live test babies at getting this walk with God, leadership, friendship, et cetera, halfway right. From it, I gained more family. So, thanks so much to **Daniel**, aka my 1st Born Son who keeps me outta jams always, to **Nicole, aka Tillaaaaay or Tillz McGillz** who can talk for an extra two hours in the car just because, to **Ephraim, aka my Bittles** who is legit just my guy (and our honorary member **Shani aka Mcani** my original PIC), to **Lasha aka LashBash** who is down for whatever even if I'm getting on her nerves, and to **Gary Andre aka Thee General or Uncle Big Dre** who protected and loved us from jump. We traveled the world, well just a few states, but it was awesomeness, and I love you all!

A special thank you also goes out to the **Unity Church of Jesus Christ** (UCJC) family. Unity was the training ground I needed when God wanted to learn me something. The relationships, friendships, and mentorships that have stemmed from the time we spent in State College are invaluable. There are many of you who took us in and we are grateful. To the **JohnsonFam**, the **Farmers**, and especially the **BarnesFam**...thank you so much!! And **Aunt Di**, thank you for always seeing beyond what I felt. Man I miss your laugh! I love my SC fam!

To *Kisha aka KDub aka Kish*...gyrl, don't even get me started. I love you! God is so DOPE for putting us in the same place accidentally on purpose. LOL! You and *Eric* are family forever, and my nieces and nephews, too, of course. Thanks so much to my big brosef, *Corey*, and his beautiful wife, *Nikki*, for being the bestest! Big bro you've known me since I was like seven! I don't have enough space to say how tight we are. And how befitting...you came through when it was time to snag my BooThing! You guys have always been there for us. And Nikki...best mom ever! I love y'all and hug the kids for me.

Much love and respect to my little sister, *Lil Bitz aka Nicole*. You are an amazing young woman who helped me grow up and take responsibility for life at a crucial stage in my development process. I'm still trying to become a better version of my yesterday self. I have no clue why you trust me with your life, but I don't think I've broken too much. LOL! To *Deshawn aka Favorite*, thank you for supporting me before, after, and during the times when you realized I was a little to the left. You've always been so selfless, what a great trait! You taught me, when we were just teenagers, that being young and on fire for the Lord was OKAY. Thank you for that! Although we're cousins it's like you're my little brother. Love you!!!

Jimmy aka James, you inspire me daily, and I'm so glad to see how you've grown in the Lord. You looked out for the cookout during some low points in my life and I'm appreciative. Thank you so much, *Lani bka Yalanda*, for allowing me to face myself and make the necessary changes to be a better friend and sister. *DEB* was the greatest gift ever, and I'm grateful to see her grow. To *Rich*, my hunni bunni, I adore you! By you being your best self, I can be my best self. You're a rare and precious stone. I will always cherish our bond.

To *TLynn*, I just have to say that you knew me while I was yet still learning who I was. You have consistently been there, and you and *Curtis* are irreplaceable. My *Morgan Puddin' Pie* brings me so much joy! I love you guys and thank you for never looking at me sideways for being unapologetically me. To *Tone, aka Troy Sr.*, you and I are like twins. How did God do that? This "thank you" could be a long dissertation. I will practice self-control. Besides, you already know. I love you and the fam, for real! Let *SarBear* and my nephews know that I send plenty of hugz and kissz to them.

I love you, *KP and Honey Badger/BP, aka Pastor Keith and Lady Tina*, because you sincerely [insert tears and temporary combustion] ...just thank you!

KP, you were the big brosef God replanted in my world when I almost lost hope in man. We met when I was 12 years old (shoutout to big sis and Mom, rest well Papa Pelz). I got to watch you take the music industry by storm, and then boom...we are back like we never left. The point is that you've been the same. You, BP, and my little people ROCK!!! Tell **Zay** to keep being dope and let **Caleb** know he made the credits.

To **La'Nique, aka LaKesha**, I can't. We were reunited and it was way better than good. You add to any person's life that you're a part of and I'm just honored that God allowed you and I to be in each other's company on a trillion types of levels. I love you and thank you! Give **RonniePooh** and **Auntie** a hug and a kiss for me! #combusting #241Sisters4Life

* * * * *

To the beautiful fruits of my womb, **Buddy and Pretty Gyrl**, thank you for loving mommy even when I was crazy. Some say I still am, but the jury's out on that one. You two are the reason why I fight so hard to be authentically me. I want you to see that you, too, can accomplish ANYTHING you set your minds to. You are breaths of fresh air, and I will always love you until my heart ceases to beat.

Words of Wisdom to you Prince and Princess: Never settle or say, "I can't," never be less than who God made you, never compromise yourselves or your beliefs, never look back...always forward, and ALWAYS keep God FIRST. You are the Lord's words fulfilled, and there is hope and promise in you both. Purpose and Destiny are synonymous with the names **Vidal Darnell and Reid Karielle**... believe that. Oh, and don't ever let anyone "allow" you to be great...remember... you were BORN that way! You don't need permission.

* * * * *

And last, but never least, **Husband, aka Juan, Darnell Jaxon, Daddy**, and all your other names that I'll keep private, you are a precious gift that only God could give to me. You have watched me mature, fail, win, disappoint, grow, annoy (mainly you), love, hate, and everything in between. You often tell me that the vows we shared were not between the two of us, but that I was and am the benefactor of the commitment you made to God. Praise Him!

Sometimes, you have led our household without knowing what the outcomes would be, but you always did it with Holy Spirit guiding and keeping you. The adversity that we'd face seemed small because you depended on God even in your distrust. My faith grew because I was and still am in an environment that is conducive to being sensitive to the voice of Lord. You've never judged me or made me feel less than, and even when God elevated us, you remained humble. Even now, you continue to do what GOD says to do.

You are the example men need. You are my *BooThing* for always and forever, and I can't wait to see how God rewards you on this earth and Heaven for your diligence and obedience. #ThankMeLater IJS

* * * * *

Now that I got that off my heart, enjoy this journey of faith the Lord brought and is still bringing me through. May the words and the lessons learned not only force you to self-examine, but may it impress on your heart the need to grow in a deeper relationship with God, our Father. May God bless you and keep you until we meet again. I love you guys for real!

Sonya

Foreword

The first time I met Sonya Sessoms, I was introduced to her vibrant smile and spirit before I knew her name. Drawn to the fire of her personality, our friendship was inevitable, especially once I understood where that fire came from and how she has used every ember to burn off anything that would get in the way of what God has for her. In the work that I do with leaders, I am constantly pushing individuals to understand their "why" in order to fuel their passion and impact. Sonya has harnessed both of those in How I Faithed It Over. The source for her fervent faith and infectious love of others is outlined chapter by chapter for the reader to understand how she passed through, pressed in and crossed over devastating situations, hurt, doubt, and haters.

Similar to our fiery phone calls, sister chats, and hearty laughs, you are able to hear Sonya's heart and voice so clearly in the pages that it's like she is sitting next to you with a cup of coffee, saying "Girl, let me tell you...". But as only a seasoned woman of God can do, she filled that chat with concrete strategies and non-negotiable accountability by challenging the reader to be bold, unwavering, and steadfast within their faith walk. Sonya's ability to be no-nonsense and completely real has made our friendship a priceless gift, and this part of her character has transferred to the steps of this faith walk through Sonya's vulnerable moments, stories of God's grace, and understanding of intimacy in relationships with human beings and God. She doesn't sugar-coat the complexity of intimate relationships; but as I have often needed to hear and understand, she reinforces the truth that a relationship with God may "rock your boat," but He'll always get you to the shore.

> *Faith is taking the first step even when you don't see the whole staircase. ~ Martin Luther King, Jr.*

Sonya's story and daily walk are a living testament for me of what God is probably just waiting to blow our minds with if we trust Him, step out, and get obedient. So many people struggle with navigating fear. The key to unlocking fear is locking into the power of faith. Our God has placed over 8,000 promises within our reach. He only wants us to take Him at His Word and leap into all the possibilities in front of us. God has promised to meet our every need, but that promise comes with the condition that we trust Him. Each one of us can live knowing that our lives do not have to be based on what the world has said, what our past has revealed, or any label that has been placed on us, but instead, on what the Word of God says about us. We are fearfully and wonderfully made, and God has an incredible plan for our lives. But knowledge isn't power until you put action to it, so as Sonya would say, "Do you trust God or don't you?" Trust Him and get moving.

Dr. Veirdre Jackson
Living Strong Consulting, LLC

Preface

For eons, people have asked me to write a book, and I marveled at the fact that what I had to say even mattered. For real, like who cares to hear my story? It turns out that God said it was TIME. Welcome to the beginning of something dope.

I grew up in a typical middle-class family in Philadelphia. Although I lost my father at a young age, my "bonus dad" stepped in and helped my mother raise me. I was in a two-parent home until about 11th grade, and although my parents remained married, we lived separately. Through their separation, I learned what strength was all about. My mother would work like a madwoman, but I never missed an opportunity; she afforded me a life of spoiledness. She was the role model I had hoped I grew to be like someday. Because of her, I wanted to the best ME I could be.

However, I suffered from pleasing people at a young age, even though it appeared that I had it all together. I was an only child who had no real friends, except those I'd met in school, and the road to finding myself was all about trial and error. When I got to the 6th grade, I gave my life to the Lord. It was one of my favorite memories, indeed. Like most new believers, I didn't fully understand what that meant. Still, I knew the decision to be "different" was going to be right up my alley.

As I grew in Christ, I experienced challenges with sin, self-identity, friendship ups and downs, and a myriad of other problems that many young women face, but during that process, I realized that I was dope. I can't tell you when that notion clicked for me, but it did, and it was almost like I became a new person. In addition to loving the Lord, I found friends who were willing to stand by me through the trials that real life would eventually bring my family and me. I made connections with individuals who did right by me and not harm, so being set apart and fearfully and wonderfully made looked great on your girl.

I found my voice of independence, of "girl power," of being unique and loving everything that encompassed who I was. I began turning into a little boss lady and sincerely admired the old me for producing the woman I was becoming. Honestly, God was with me every step of the way, but it was in my college years that I noticed what a genuine relationship looked like, and I've been loving the Father and trying my best to be who He called me to be ever since. So this "something dope" is just a small glimpse of very pivotal and life-altering moments I've endured. Moments that I pray will cause you to do some introspection and grow in your relationship with Christ, like I am still doing.

My story is not a new one; it's just custom made for me. God made me different. He handcrafted me, just like He made you. I love the fact that everyone on this tremendously "gihugic" earth has a story to tell, and a responsibility to share what they have learned. What you have to say can help your family, friends, or someone you have never met. Stories are essential for our life's lessons. We take our cue from the most excellent storyteller to have walked this land, Jesus Christ.

His stories, better known as parables, keep us captivated and positioned for consistent growth and learning. He told the most informative, challenging, and thought-provoking stories. As a result, lives changed, healings and miracles took place, and the world was allowed to have a relationship with God, the Father, the Son, and the Holy Ghost. I'm grateful for each opportunity He has ever placed in my path. I am thankful for every sin I've committed because it allowed me to feel what real love was, when grace and mercy overshadowed my imperfections.

So my journey, which is still underway, has been a doozy at times. I wholeheartedly know that when folks ask, "How'd you do it?" my response is an overwhelming, "But God!" I'm a bona fide Faith Stalker. What is that you ask? It's a person who stealthily takes one blind step at a time. So please sit back and enjoy this dopeness and let's grow together.

Faith Stalking 101 is now in session...

*Faith Stalking: to stealthily take one blind step at a time.

1

Faithing Ain't Easy

> DON'T EVER LOSE YOUR ZEAL, YOUR FERVOR FOR GOD, AND THE THINGS THAT CONCERN HIM. JESUS POSSESSED FERVOR FOR US ALL THE WAY TO THE CROSS. WE HAVE NO EXCUSE.

The Bible says in Hebrews 11 verse 6:

"⁶And without faith it is impossible to please him, for whoever would draw near to God must believe that he exists and that he rewards those who seek him."

If I am honest, I don't think I fully understood this verse until I got to college. If you ask my mother, though, she will tell stories about my childhood years when I would say faith-like things. She said I'd say phrases like, "If it's in God's will..." and "If God won't do it..." and her favorite one was, "You just gotta believe it, and God will make a way."

She insists that I was beyond my years and that I'd encourage everyone I met. At such a young age, however, I couldn't comprehend what faith was or even what a relationship with God looked like, so to me, it was something that the Father allowed me to "unknowingly" experience. I couldn't quite articulate what it was or why I even had it. I do remember feeling like God wasn't always faithful to me. I had experienced real loss in my life before I was old enough to understand what "family" was and how it was supposed to look.

My biological father, Stanley, lost his battle to kidney failure when I was just six years old. After learning this news as a child, I don't think I ever processed that I had an earthly father who loved me and wanted me to be my best me, just like my mother did. And every little girl indeed needs her father. Moments in my young adult years into adulthood were awkward because I never had my father, who would give me wisdom from a male's perspective. Now I eventually would be blessed with a stepfather, but there's something special about the parents who created you and how they pour into your life.

Many would not agree with the idea that your birth parents are the only ones who can do the pouring. I would not disagree with you, but I'd strongly suggest that your bloodline, generational patterns, habits, issues, and more are only revealed (or concealed in some families) by the parents who birthed you. Now some of you have never had the opportunity to meet your birth parents because you could be adopted. In this instance, you can't "trace" your lineage to find out about your family's medical history or even begin to unpack character traits, flaws and all, beyond what the social worker has on file.

Others have parents who just decided to choose other things to occupy their time, and maybe you were raised by a family member. And in all our situations, I'm confident we felt alone and perhaps even carried the weight of the same type of void. The feeling like you were cheated out of your "good" thing or at least the opportunity to know why you act the way you do, why you look the way you do, and the list goes on and on. In life, both little boys and little girls need to have both parents present, biological ones, or those God gifts, to help foster a balance in their upbringing.

I had to learn that when that wasn't possible, my best plan was to take advantage of my bonus parent, my gift from God, and learn and grow as much as I could. God even blessed me with a father-in-love who was hands down, one of the greatest men I knew. I had my grandfather, aka Pop-Pop, aka Rev. Noah Reid, II still with me who pushed me beyond measure, and I had my Uncle Victor, who was instrumental in my upbringing. So I wasn't without a "father." I just couldn't get over the days I'd ponder how amazing it would've been to know what my biological father was like when he was younger.

I'd always wonder if I was like him and his side of the family. I would dream about what life would've been like for me if he had been present. Unfortunately for me, I was too young to connect with my dad to know what I was missing. But was it me "missing out" when God ordered my steps? It wasn't until my father-in-love passed in 2012, then my Pop-Pop in 2014, along with my stepfather that same year that the feeling of void crept right back up. So in the spring of 2017, not knowing that my Uncle Victor would pass away later that year, I began a more real search for my biological father's family and any children he may have left behind.

It was my 4th attempt at trying to locate my biological family, and this time I was hoping he was a rolling stone so I could have that sister or brother I believed I needed to get through life. Don't judge me. From this longing and intense digging, I came to learn that his mother and father were both deceased and that I was his only child. He was his mother's only child. And guess what? She also was an only child. Wow! Although connecting to this side of my family looked like a lost cause, I asked God to please bring closure, and He did.

I was able to locate my grandmother's first cousin. He told me that my dad was super smart, loved reading, was funny, and made sure education was always first. That meant I was more like my dad than I knew. He also received an honorable discharge from the military, which indicated that he had some sort of discipline. During this search for my father, my mom found many things, but my favorite keepsake was a hand-written note that professed his love, not only for my mother, but for me as well. I instantly received confirmation that he wanted us to be one big happy family and that he loved us both. I received great facts about a man that I can only remember vaguely. God instantly redeemed the time.

Somewhere in my life, I had to believe that something good would come out of all the challenges I faced. I had to tap into the strength my mother showed, the trust my grandparents preached about, and the love I felt each time I had the opportunity to wake up to another day filled with new mercies. Always having faith, as my mother put it, would mean that I trusted God without wavering and believed God had a more excellent plan. "Always" is a constant type of word, one I teach my children to avoid. "Always" and "never" leave little to no room for change, but she stands by the fact that I always had faith.

God's hand and plan were ALWAYS over my life from the very beginning. That is a constant that will never change. Maturing in life and in my relationship with Christ made me see that the word best described as "my remarkable knack to see God in every situation" was my ability to approach life with *fervor* . The Old Testament's definition of fervent is from the word *fervere* , which is Latin for "to boil," which also means "to burn." Let's look at Leviticus 6:12-13:

> *"12 And the fire upon the altar shall be burning in it; it shall not be put out: and the priest shall burn wood on it every morning, and lay the burnt offering in order upon it; and he shall burn thereon the fat of the peace offerings. 13 The fire shall ever be burning upon the altar; it shall never go out."*

Some scholars will say that this fire is the same "fire" or "might" that you see throughout the Old Testament. I'm confident we can point to many scriptures, but one I enjoy is Psalm 63:1:

> *"1 God, you are my God; earnestly I seek you; my soul thirsts for you; my flesh faints for you, as in a dry and weary land where there is no water."*

"Earnest" is a synonym for fervor/fervent. This verse simply means that our souls should never cease to burn for God and His laws. We need to be purposeful and intentional about seeking Him out. Are you intentional? Do you have fervor?

Now without making this a lesson in languages, let's look at zeō, Strong's #2204. Pronounced "dzeh'-o," it's a primary verb meaning to be hot (boil, of liquids, or glow, of solids), i.e. (figuratively) be fervid (earnest): -be fervent. In Thayer's Greek Lexicon, it means to boil with heat or be hot, like boiling water. Metaphorically, we have

1) used of boiling anger, love, zeal, for what is good or bad
2) fervent in spirit, said of zeal for what is good.

Hopefully, you're starting to pick up what's being put down. One more word, ek-tenés, Strong's #1618. It's pronounced "ek-ten-ace'" and means intent, constant, strenuous, intense; met: earnest, zealous. If we turn in our Bibles to 1 Peter 4:8,

> *⁸ Above all, keep loving one another earnestly, since love covers a multitude of sins."*

we will see that we should stretch our love out not just for God and ourselves but also for others. Go figure.

Let's just keep a picture of the cross in your minds. See Jesus outstretched, nailed to the cross, which was not only the ultimate sacrifice, but God's display of the type of love that we should strive for daily. John 15:13 says:

> *¹³ Greater love has no one than this, that someone lay down his life for his friends."*

We also find in Romans 12:11 that we should be fervent in spirit,

> *¹¹ Do not be slothful in zeal, be fervent in spirit, serve the Lord."*

These verses translate as us being on fire for the precepts of the Father. This kind of intensity takes practice, no doubt, but Holy Spirit dwells within us to support us as we try our best to "keep the faith." Hebrews 12:1-2 says:

> *¹ Therefore, since we are surrounded by such a great cloud of witnesses, let us throw off everything that hinders and the sin that so easily entangles. And let us run with perseverance the race marked*

out for us,[2] fixing our eyes on Jesus the pioneer and perfecter of faith.
For the joy set before him he endured the cross, scorning its shame,
and sat down at the right hand of God."

This is fervor at its best. Despite what may distract us, despite what may trip us up in this life, and even despite ourselves, we will do the will of the Lord. Be admonished to stay on the course that was tailor-made for you. And the word "race" simply denotes that we have to keep going. We shouldn't quit, we should press in and press on because the goal is simple, to be with our Heavenly Father.

What better example of faith do we have than Jesus himself? He is not only the originator, the head honcho, the greatest ever to do it, but He allowed us to receive grace and mercy because of His fervent mission to fulfill the will of his Father on the cross. If this doesn't give you yet another reminder that, as a believer, we should exude passion and an intense desire to seek God, I'm not sure what would. Do me a favor, won't you? Grab your cell phone or hop on your computer/tablet right quick. Go to Google and type in the word fervent.

Let's look at the definition, you know that's how a lot of pastors start their sermons off right? They provide you with a whole host of meanings. I am guilty of doing that too, but it just helps you get the point in plain English. Sometimes knowing the definition of a word or twelve will open up a new way of you understanding the Word of the Lord. So don't judge us too much.

Okay, so we're all at Google's site, we've typed in "fervent," and we see that the archaic definition is "hot, burning or glowing." It's rather cool knowing that an outdated description still works today and will continue to work until Jesus comes back to the Earth. The point is simple. We cannot live life without intentionally seeking after God.

We should do so with joy, happiness, and zeal, fervently. I've never seen an unhappy child in a candy store, unless her mom and dad told her she had TOO MUCH candy. To be honest, we should resemble a kid in the candy store when being intentional about God, learning, growing, praying, loving. Having fervor extends across the row too. We should seek out ways to bless others as our Father has blessed us. There's nothing like having a whole bag of treats and not sharing it with anybody else. We can't be stingy with our God.

I recall the very first time I told a stranger about the power of the Lord. I had to be about 13, and I was on the six (6) bus, back in Philly. I didn't really get nervous talking to people, but this time I was a little apprehensive because the young lady clearly looked defeated and almost unapproachable, but I sat next to her anyway. I began to ask her how her day was and just told her how God loved her and that He always works it out for His children. I had no clue why those were the words I chose, but she smiled, and tears began to fall from her face, it was then that I knew my fervor was not just for me, but it was contagious. It was meant for others as well.

For the remainder of my ride, we laughed and talked as much as we could since I was so young, but she was sure to tell me that I made her day and that it would INDEED be alright. She also told me to always trust in the Lord. The moral of the story is that we have to stay fervent in our life's daily pursuits. It's all about Faith, no half-stepping.

— ·· — ·· — ·

<u>Your Lifework...yes...lifework, not homework:</u>

Reflect on a moment in time when you can recall the Lord desiring more from you. Some of us may admit that this is a daily occurrence, but there is one moment in all of our lives, where we can vividly hear the voice of the Lord asking us if that was all we had to give to Him. It's moments like those, when we receive our heavenly nudge, that should force us to have our hearts ablaze for the Master. Starting this week, seek the Lord with zeal, excitement, and a fervent heart, and watch God answer the call.

Get your pen and paper aka your journals ready to write what He says. He's never had an outage and always has excellent service, so you might as well call on Him right where you are.

2

Faith, No Half-Stepping

**" HAVE YOU EVER STEPPED OFF THE CURB WITHOUT CHECK-
ING FOR A CAR FIRST? NO? WELL GOOD. THAT MEANS YOU
PAY ATTENTION TO YOUR SURROUNDINGS, THE VEHICLES,
THE TRAFFIC LIGHTS, OTHER PEDESTRIANS, ETC. IN LIFE,
GOD SENDS US MANY SIGNS AND SIGNALS TOO. MAKE SURE
YOU PAY CLOSE ATTENTION. "**

I can attest to the fact that being fervent comes with practice, and the amount of zeal you possess is in direct correlation with how long you've been a believer. I would say that in your younger years of being saved, depending on how old you were when you accepted Christ, you were elated because of this "newness." You are reading and praying daily, just living the good ol' life, but then year 8 or 9 hits (maybe 4/5), and you become bombarded with life's issues that are sometimes dauntingly discouraging. A few more years later, you're questioning God, yourself, your existence, and everyone you come in contact with. That's called the "living" phase.

Nobody ever told you the narrow path would be quite this exasperating, exhausting, and unexciting at moments in your life, but it is. That's when your fervor turns into "fer." Some people jump ship when the going gets tough, but I'm grateful Jesus endured His trials and tests because we are now able to have freedom in Him.

Now, if you didn't decide to denounce the whole religion by the time you're well into living life, your "-vor" comes back. You realize that what you are building in life is a healthy relationship that will have ebbs and flows, hills and valleys, highs and lows. So keep that enthusiasm and stroll down memory lane, with me... let's stop at my high school years.

I was coming into a new season of life, almost adulthood. The time in many of our lives where we begin to smell ourselves and test boundaries because we feel like we're grown, almost, part of the way. We feel like we're old enough to live our own lives...why? And we feel like everyone around us should just get it...duh! LOL! I was also not exempt from testing those limits with my parents, but for me, I can vividly see where the shift began to take place in my spiritual life more than anything.

At home, God was always the center of our lives, but I had joined my cousin's community choir with my mom (because I was finally old enough...see, getting up there) and noticed that these young people loved God for seriousness. I mean, crying out, shouting, speaking in these weird languages, and I was like, "WHOA! I'm too young for this deepness." Simultaneously I was headed to the absolute, hands down, unequivocally, indubitably, greatest high school in the entire world, the mighty Philadelphia High School for Girls. (Shout out to the c/o of 1997...241 what's good?) HashtagJudgeSomeoneElse.

In Girls' High, I remember that I had officially begun a wrestling match with myself. I was trying to discover who Sonya was. Most of us, even as full-blown grown adults, struggle with this very same thing, our identity. So here I am, in high school, "grown," trying to determine what type of individual I wanted to be in this world.

Did I have it in me to be a good friend? Did I have what it took to stay true to myself and what I believed when faced with peer pressure? Would I have what it took to profess my love for God always? After posing all of those questions, I realized I didn't always display the proper response to others. Quite honestly, I fell short many, many times. If I could be frank, I enjoyed being a little reckless here and there, and I enjoyed living a lukewarm existence despite what the Bible says. In Revelation 3:15-16 it reads:

> *"15 I know your works: you are neither cold nor hot. Would that you were either cold or hot! 16 So, because you are lukewarm, and neither hot nor cold, I will spit you out of my mouth..."*

Let's pause on that scripture. Reread it if you must. The Bible clearly states that our works are KNOWN, so yes, the creeping, the cussing, the drinking (underage), the partying, the unruly behavior, the disrespect for yourself and others, all of that, including the moments we are alone and straight out of control, are seen. And even when you read those words and grasp its meaning, it still doesn't allow us to win the battle against our flesh at times. It's a daily process. These "flesh tents," as my husband calls them, are the reason for some of our demises.

I partially cared about these scriptures and, at the same time, didn't care at all. In high school, I was right where many of us were. Right smack dab in the middle of "am I saved or ain't I"...in real life. It wasn't like God wasn't trying His best to keep me focused on those living out loud for Him in school moments. I mean, I had great examples. One young lady would proclaim the name of Jesus every day, and if she wasn't talking about Him, she was singing a song about Him. BOLDNESS!

She was not concerned about how people viewed her and was cool with folks knowing who she served. I used to think that I was on fire for God but realized that maybe I was on smoke for Him and not fully ablaze. My friends knew I was saved and that I was a "church girl," but being a legit extrovert for God wasn't "my thing." You had to know me personally.

How many of you reading/listening to this know that God will always provide a way of escape for you? *insert shout here* Go on ahead and shout, I'll wait. I ask this question because I believe the Lord is always lifetimes ahead of us. Duh! He IS the Creator! You see, high school was the perfect place for me. I could love God "under the radar" and live how I wanted to live without being put on blast, or so I thought.

That hiding lasted all but one or two months of my freshman year, because He sent me the only person in the entire world with the name, Aronissa, to infiltrate my plan. Shout out to my big brosef Marvin for marrying my sister and changing her name and her life. As I digress, listen to me carefully, when I tell you that God knitted Aronissa and me together forever, I mean FOREVER, however long that will be. He allowed me to hit the big sister jackpot with this gem.

She instantly received a nickname. I believe all of your close friends should have one. I have several for her, but my main one is NissBiss. Man, I'm so blessed to have her in my life! Legit blessed. This woman of God was so mighty to me back then. She still is today, but when you're young in your natural and spiritual life and what looks like a giant enters the scene, you pay ATTENTION.

Just two years and grades older/higher than me, this young woman meant business, I mean she even wore suits to school. Who was doing that in 1993? She was also the first one to introduce me to "business casual." Haaaahaaaaa...go ahead, all of you can laugh. She was walking around in jeans, shoes, and suit jackets. I was like whaaaaaaat????

NissBiss was a leader, natural born. She was the Junior Class President when I met her during my freshman year, so she was a big deal to me. She held that title in her senior year as well. To make a long story semi-short, she was who I wanted to be. As an only child, you often struggle with who you are because you are so used to being alone.

You don't have anyone to bounce ideas off of, anyone to debate with, anyone who will listen to your dreams and goals, it's just you and your parents. So I welcomed this example of a young person who was straight up dopeness in my eyes. Aronissa was the queen of "firsts" too in high school. She started a gospel choir and petitioned the student government for what was the first and probably the only Virgins' Club, yes, a club full of virgins (and those rehabilitated).

I mean, she was A-mazing! I can't tell you when, during that first year of high school, I met her, but I do know that I was watching her, and I loved her without even knowing she was that dope outside of school too. She was just a great example. This girl was also teaching and preaching! To be honest, spending time with her started to be the highlight of my day in real life.

Girls' High was admired for their big sister/little sister program. Every freshman who came in would be assigned a big sister who was a senior. It was nothing short of amazing to have this kind of mentorship. My cousin was my "senior" sister, and Aronissa was my "junior" big sister...I had sisters in every class though, too many to name. LOL! My senior big sister taught me how to be low key. She was one of the most flyest dressers I knew, she still is, and she never raised her voice. No seriously, never.

She was a scholar and artistic, which let me know that being interested in the arts was okay. Together, they poured into me, not just on a spiritual level, but on a "BE YOU" type of level. I don't believe I ever got a chance to really thank my "senior" big sister, so "Thank you, wherever you are!!! You were fashion-forward in the '90s, stuck to your trends, loved God, and taught me how to be independent. I love you!" I paid attention to all of the young women who poured into me.

I went into my sophomore year, saying goodbye and many blessings to my cousin and watching NissBiss shine in her senior year. This second year of high school challenged me because I was still a member of the community choir outside of school (shout out to my cousin John and Divine Praise), which was a constant reminder that living for God should be at the forefront of everything I did from day to day. I was learning about the word "loyal." I'm sure I can write another book on that. I was trying to keep sexual sin in the back of my mind. Lord, help me.

Juan, affectionately called Husband throughout this book, was my boyfriend back then and was just as hot as he is now. I'm just saying (IJS). I had to dig deep to see if there was a leader somewhere in my belly. I had to pay attention this year, and I noticed the ease I had when it came to focusing on God. But when you have your built-in "guides," everything is simple. Now let's fast forward to the year after NissBiss graduated. Junior year!

I was successful in winning the election for Junior Class President, so I kind of felt like I picked up where she left off. What I was missing, though, was God's "voice." I might as well couple my senior year in here too and let you all know that 241 also voted me in to act as their Senior Class President. It was nothing short of a real honor to serve. These years also presented me with many challenges. I was confronted with having a more substantial level of responsibility and had to walk in integrity FOR REAL.

The tug on my spirit-woman became stronger. Thankfully God sent a family friend who was that still voice of balance. God was, again, trying to get me outside of myself and into Him. Now don't get me wrong, I had other friends in high school. Shout out to those women who know who they are. I don't have time to talk about those Club Dances nights, the competitions and performances, the cookouts, the trips, the friend lessons, and all of that. It would honestly take me a minute to get all of those moments in. I cherished those years. Our class sponsor was also instrumental in helping me see beyond what was in front of me. I know I used to drive her crazy.

Now, for as long as I can remember, God was trying to grab my attention long enough to change my life permanently. The women I mentioned at length stuck out the most when I pinpoint pivotal people that God sent to ignite the passion I now have for Him and His word. I felt like further clarification was needed because all of my friends/big sisters/little sisters in high school, some I still have relationships with, taught me more than I could ever write. I didn't always live my best life as a believer, but believe me, each young lady back then was a vital part of my growth. I was in my character-building stage. My "do you have faith or naw" phase.

I'm grateful for every experience. You don't even know how it has shaped my outlook in so many facets of my adult life. Thank you, women of 241. I must also give an honorable mention and thanks to 238, 239, 240, and our little sisters of 244. What I grasped in those four short years was the importance of paying attention to all of my surroundings. All of my experiences, my highs, my lows, my great, my horrible, and sometimes even my embarrassing moments were necessary to get me to this point. It's true. Everything does happen for a reason.

Let's switch gears. When you're driving in your car, you're supposed to pay attention, right? You need to do many things at once. You need to watch other drivers, watch yourself, watch the lights and traffic signs, watch for pedestrians and other things like pets that may run into the street, wait for bike riders, watch for potholes, and so much more. Therefore, paying attention requires a tremendous amount of focus. You need to be able to avoid distractions that will come to you. If you haven't noticed yet, this is a book about faith, so let's look at an all-familiar story in the good book, the story of Noah.

Noah was instructed by God to build an ark. Some scholars will also submit that Noah must have had a profound relationship with God, and I will be inclined to agree because the Bible says that he found grace with God. Other translations say favor, but he did not have a working knowledge of how to build an ark. I'm almost sure he was like, "Build what God?" As we read the directions, we find that God was particular. Genesis 6:14-16 says:

"¹⁴Make yourself an ark of gopher wood. Make rooms in the ark, and cover it inside and out with pitch. ¹⁵This is how you are to make it: the length of the ark 300 cubits, its breadth 50 cubits, and its height 30 cubits. ¹⁶Make a roof for the ark, and finish it to a cubit above, and set the door of the ark in its side. Make it with lower, second, and third decks."

Noah had extremely detailed instructions. I mean, God told him exactly what kind of wood to use. Now, what if Noah decided that he wasn't going to pay attention during God's delivery of the materials and procedures? Those waters would've raged, and the Ark would not have sustained the impact. That means we would not be here today, so shout out to Noah for being a man concerned about the details! No, we should be reminded of his keen knack to pay attention to but one voice, and that was God's.

What I pray you're grasping is that faith requires all our attention. We can't operate at 50% and expect God to give 100%. And the myth that if we take one step, God takes two is nowhere in the Bible. We offer our best to the best, period. We're a trip that way.

The attitude that screams, "just let me just go to church on Sundays and skip worship as my actual lifestyle." How about, "let me just make two-thirds of Bible study and only spend time in the Word when instructed to read it," yep, I'm on a roll now. Or my favorite, since I loved being lukewarm, "let me just live this ratchet life being sure to ask for forgiveness because that's the real key, God always forgives, right?!" Oh, and "let me only pray when I need something because God will show up on time and make a way outta no way." Won't He do it? Oh, oh, and "let me just say thank you when Jesus gets me out of a jam, because daily thanks for the significant air I breathe isn't required...only when I get those breaks and blessings." Ha! *steps off of soapbox*

In all seriousness, we as believers often lack focus and miss the moments when God demands we pay attention. We miss directions and instructions and realize that once we arrive at our destinations, our boats can't float in a puddle, let alone a whole body of water...BUT GOD! Our heavenly Father, in all of His awesomeness, allows us more time to rebuild the boat, but we don't take into account the amount of time wasted. The time we squandered trying to do things on our own.

Now that we're older, our lives have changed. They are different from when the initial directives came to us, and we get into that "if I only paid attention back then" mentality. This type of stinking thinking prolongs your progress. We miss opportunities. We miss blessings and the chance to bless others; we just miss it. Our churches today are lacking the attention they need to help the lost in their very own sanctuaries.

God is giving direction, Jesus is interceding, Holy Spirit indwells us waiting for us to seek guidance, and we don't even call on them for their help because "we got it." We've lost our way, and our ability to focus has diminished. The world needs to wake up from its slumber. We need a fresh wind, but if we aren't paying attention when God speaks, we will remain stagnant.

God's challenging us to wake up!!! We cry out day in and day out for a healing word, for a Rhema word, instructions and guidance, but God says, "Did you speak to this mountain in your life? Did you follow the directives I gave that would've prevented this present stagnation?" My suggestion to you is simple, grab hold of what you "missed" and ask the Lord for a quick reset, right where you are.

God didn't create us to bear so much weight. The number of pounds we often put on ourselves because we haven't taken the time out to become pros at being attentive is astounding. Start today! Psalm 55:22 reads,

> *"²²Cast your burden on the Lord, and he will sustain you; he will never permit the righteous to be moved."*

Therefore, get rid of that shoulda, coulda, woulda mindset RIGHT NOW!

We need to grab hold of the favor that's rightfully ours. We get that by following the rules we receive. Grab a mirror, look at yourself, and say, "PAY ATTENTION!!!" Faith ain't no joke!

— · · — · · — ·

Your Lifework:

Pause for a moment.

Take a deep breath.

Inhale.

Exhale.

Now forgive yourself.

Many instances often haunt us in life where we know God was instructing us, but we were so busy being "ourselves" that we weren't paying attention. Maybe you lost focus during your partying years, or drug-abusing years, or during your toxic relationship and friendship years, or right now in your "it's too late" years. God gives us guidelines on purpose, and that's why He created you for His purpose, ON purpose. It's never too late to PAY ATTENTION, so grab your pen and journal and start again. He has your full attention now. You got this! Remember that Philippians chapter one verse six says,

"And I am sure of this, that he who began a good work in you will bring it to completion at the day of Jesus."

3

Faith Ain't No Joke

" THERE IS NO RELATIONSHIP WITHOUT INTIMACY.
EVEN WITH THE MOST ELEMENTARY CONNECTION, CLOSE-
NESS AND BONDS ARE NECESSARY FOR PROGRESSION.
DON'T LIVE A CLOSED-OFF LIFE WITH A FATHER
WHO KNOWS ALL, SEES ALL, AND QUITE HONESTLY WANTS
THE VERY BEST FOR YOU.
MAKE INTIMACY A REGULAR PART OF
YOUR SPIRITUAL ROUTINE. WITHOUT IT, YOU DON'T HAVE
MUCH OF A RELATIONSHIP. "

We're clear now, right? We are still talking about faith. You'll realize that this one tiny, but crucial, piece of a believer's walk with Christ is difficult to maintain. It's a fundamental aspect of our belief system. Having faith is the ability to believe in what, and who, is not seen. Better yet, the Bible says in John chapter 4 that God is spirit,

> *"23 But the hour is coming, and is now here, when the true worshipers will worship the Father in spirit and truth, for the Father is seeking such people to worship him. 24 God is spirit, and those who worship him must worship in spirit and truth."*

This verse solidifies the well-known fact that we won't "see" God until Jesus comes back a second time (aka the Second Coming). I understand that such a candid book may not be all you need to have and keep the faith, but prayerfully it's an aid for you to continue to press your way. I can attest to the notion that this ability to live daily, believing in the unseen, gets complicated at times. Now faith is the assurance of things hoped for, the conviction of things not seen (Hebrews 11:1).

Husband and I talked a little about this simple but complex verse that begins with the word "now." As an adverb, *now* is defined as "at the present time or moment," and as a conjunction, it means as "a consequence of the fact." Choose one you like and let's roll with it, because they're both applicable in this verse. What about substance?

When you hear that word, you immediately think of something with volume, something you can touch and hold. How is that possible when faith is the substance of things hoped for, meaning things we do not have, but wish for? Have you taken the time to dissect what this verse tells us? We've already covered that faith requires us to believe in what we cannot see. True or True? So let me take a stab at the verse in plain English.

Here's what I deduced Hebrews 11:1 says, "It's a fact, at this present time or moment, that faith is physical material from which something is made, of things, to want something to happen or be true, the evidence (something that furnishes proof; testimony) of things not seen." Too much, too soon? Yeah, I feel the same way. Faith ain't no joke! For that very reason, I'd like to focus on Intimacy.

You're probably like, oh wow, are we just jumping right into sex now? LOL! No, we are not; all intimacy is not sexual. HashtagFO-CUS. I've learned that you must speak those things that are not, as though they were. But if you've been a believer for a considerable amount of time, you may recall your pastor or teacher saying that intimacy translated is: Into-Me-See. And if you've never heard that before, you're welcome.

This rendering of the word is 100% accurate, and shout-outs go to the very first pastor who put this in the atmosphere for everyone to build on. That's what it's all about, right? Helping one another gain insight so that we can teach and interpret the Word better. We often get so caught up in wanting credit for everything that we miss the audience of ONE who gave it to us from the beginning. I won't start...that's a totally different lane that I'm not currently driving in, so let me get back on track. I honestly believe that I've heard "into me see" hundreds of times to date, and each leader has nailed the picture I'd like to try and paint.

If you use any relationship you value as a base, you'll realize that there are many levels involved. For instance, your work friends, the friends you have known for a few years, and the friends you've had since childhood all get varying amounts of information concerning your life. Each group of friends have their imaginary tiers in your head. An invisible buzzer will go off if any of these individuals try to cross lanes too quickly or before you've felt they have graduated to another friendship level. If we "kept it one hundred," as the saying goes, we have too many labels for our "friends."

We call folks associates, buddies, friends, framily (friends turned family, because blood won't make y'all any closer), like family, shoulda been homies, besties forever, something like a brother or sister, you thought we were tight, but we're only on speaking terms kind of friends, and the list goes on. The truth of the matter is that some of us have lost our fervor, our ability to pay attention, and our intimacy with God because we have the wrong people in our lives. They're called DISTRACTIONS.

We spend too much time here on this great earth entertaining people, places, and things that don't allow us to fulfill the purpose God planted in us before we were formed. Somebody say, "Distractions will kill you!" Say it one more time, "Distractions will kill you!" And I do mean literally.

Distractions not only tear us down and keep us from our destinies, but they are put in place to kill us. That's what the thief is coming to do, steal, kill, and destroy (John 10:10). And you can't be destroyed if you aren't being distracted! Maintaining focus on things and people that are beneficial to you is hard because we live in a world filled with almost every pleasantry we think we need, but if we keep our eyes on the prize, literally, God will help us with our distractions. He really will. Intimacy is crucial to the believer.

Your spouse or significant other isn't in the same category as the folks I previously mentioned. Your relationship's scope and nature should be more in-depth than the one you have with, let's say, your "bestie." If it isn't, you need to repent at this very moment and ask the Lord to restore ORDER in your life and your household... IMMEDIATELY. No friend should be on a higher plane than your spouse lest it's God, Himself. Levels are in place for a reason, and even Jesus had levels in friendship/relationships.

Don't believe me? What about James, Peter, and John? Jesus had 12 disciples, but the three men I mentioned were held near and dear to his heart. They were so tight that even at the beginning of the beginning (you'll catch it), He took with Him just Peter, James, and John (Matthew 26:37). It's almost like He had an earthly representation of the Trinity. I threw that visual in for my fellow theologians to wrestle with, dissect, and teach at Bible Study or on Sunday morning. You're welcome.

We uncover, with Jesus' lead, that it takes time to build rapport and trust, and you need evaluation time and space as well. You must decide if the individuals you surround yourself with are deserving or worthy, depending on your level of narcissism, of knowing you on a deeper level. Based on your experience with these people, you choose to move forward with a friendship and, in the case of courtship, a deep romantic relationship. During this time, you decide if this friend is a lifer or here for a season, a passerby.

You determine if this man or woman is your future or a complete and utter waste of time. You're assessing your relationships, and the terms they were built on, how they receive maintenance and nurture. Is this healthy food or junk food? Be clear, knowing that what you take in, who you spend time with, what you eat willingly, and what you allow others to feed you, is what and who you ultimately become.

I've learned that **there is no relationship without intimacy**. Please understand that there must be intimacy BEFORE there is a relationship. Again, there must be intimacy before there is a relationship. Look at the definition of intimacy, since defining words is fun and educational. Overlook the sexual meaning for now.

We're going to focus on intimacy described as "closeness of observation or knowledge of a subject." You'll also find fantastic synonyms like: friendship, togetherness, affinity, attachment, warmth, and rapport, to name a handful. I would like to think that you can't have faith if you don't know God intimately. It's almost like expecting someone to just give you a job. They don't know you! You better enjoy that interview with your resume and references in hand.

If we just met at a bare-bones level, you would probably only walk away from our initial conversation knowing my name, that I'm married, and maybe you'll squeeze my professional field out of me...maybe. Depending on how long we converse, you may come to learn that I'm a mother too, but there's no real need for me to tell you that I'm an only child, that I'm originally from Philly but just moved to Texas four years ago, and I love the color blue. Why? Because I don't know you. We just met. Why are you all in my business? LOL! If you ask me too many personal questions, I'll end the conversation early because we are not on that level.

Let's go back to that job you secured because your interview was just that awesome. What if you were the only male or female in the office? What if you were not part of the majority race in the office? Never happened to you? You see, being the only Black woman isn't unfamiliar in my field of expertise, and it's not far-fetched based on my geographical location.

I can vividly recall a position I had as a contractor. I was the only Black woman in that office (thankfully, not the entire department), and I had a makeshift desk that faced the wall. Yes, an actual wall with a humongous dry-erase board on it. When I came in for the first day, my mouth was on the floor in shawe (shock and awe), as you can imagine. I mean, you all couldn't put me at the intern's spot?

Yeah, but anyhoo, the issue I had stemmed from my co-worker wanting to debate a sensitive and racially-heavy topic. Who's talking about that during their second week of work? Not me! I pass! I mean, I wasn't moving on because I didn't have an opinion, but I hardly knew them. It was too much, waaaaaaay too soon. I prefer to talk about a few surface items first. I need to have some type of assurance that, if we're walking down a dark street, I won't get beat over the head, kicked and dragged, and then you ask me what I'm doing for lunch the next day.

No ma'am! I'll be quiet this go-round and observe my surroundings, which is an adage learned from my youth. I mean, we don't even know each other's middle names yet. And why are we having this conversation at work, anyway?! We were on the topic of my speeding ticket and somehow ended up at a black man not knowing how to select a jury for his crime. How did we get here? How? I was silent, and if you know me, you know that was extremely trying. LOL! From my very brief experience, we can extrapolate that your environment determines your comfort level.

If we were outside the workplace, maybe I would have engaged in that conversation with my co-worker. On second thought, naaaaaaaaaah. On third thought, I'd probably engage with her if we didn't have to see each other every day, keeping in mind that whatever comes out of our mouths, intentionally or unintentionally, cannot be withdrawn. A simple discussion balled up with an individual's opinions can potentially tarnish the chance we had to grow to know one another sincerely.

I wanted to paint that picture because it matters what you talk about with your new associates and how soon you reveal intimate details about your personal beliefs and opinions. Peruse the New Testament for proof. I rarely discuss any personal information in a work setting. My better-half is worse than I am. He goes to work, talks about work, and comes home.

Those who know more find out by accident, or put in the time to learn who he is as an individual. I'm sure many of you also feel that work is work and personal is personal. My question is, "But why?" Why does it matter? Why can't you just share anything you choose to strangers? Why can't you just be you and keep it real? I believe you don't divulge private nothings to folks you just met because you don't know that man or woman enough to trust them.

You've not had enough intimate encounters with them to learn that you, your feelings, and your information are all safe – being handled with the most delicate ears and hearts possible. How about husbands and wives? When you get married, you should realize that this man or woman is not only the proud recipient of your body until death, but they are also worthy of your intimacy at the most intimate level. Now that's deep.

You should get so close that you've shared stories from childhood, the good and the bad ones, some that may include abuse, molestation, and addiction, yeah, those kinds. You share moments when you had no gas or heat in your house, growing up, or how you watched your parents fist-fight and curse most of your upbringing. You tell them about the promiscuous life you led in high school. You tell them how you became a single parent at 17 or 18 years old. You peel the layers of the onion beyond what is comfortable because intimacy is uncomfortable. Folks are not out here really tryna be about that becoming ONE life. It's not easy for a reason.

You share secrets from your college years and talk about the challenges you've faced as an adult. Maybe you tried drugs before, or perhaps you wanted to commit suicide. Now it's not all bad, of course, but when you're about to walk down the aisle, the good is a given. They want to know the real you, not a polished representation of you. And by polished, I mean the representative you send with the bundles, makeup, clothes you only purchased to floss the haircut with dye to cover the holes in your beard.

Don't give out that version. Shade no shade. They want the person they will spend the rest of their lives with, even if you only had a penny in the bank. The person that values and cherishes the time spent together over their need to purchase a pair of red bottoms or a new pair of sneaks. JUST YOU!

That version of you has to be the one you fall in love with FIRST. The version you know on an intimate and personal level is who you need to present. That's a message in and of itself. Why? I'll tell you. This is how your husband/wife learns how to handle you, your feelings, and your emotions for years and years and years and years and years to come. This is how you build a marriage that lasts a lifetime versus one that lasts for a moment in time.

The divorce rate is high because too many of us are marrying representatives, the person you want everyone to think and believe you are. Let's start with being intimate with yourself so you can have a stable relationship with yourself from the beginning. I said that right. Doing this will allow you to be open and available for who

God has prepared for you and only you. You'll be able to find your custom-tailored partner. That's what's up!

One of my favorite R&B artists wrote a song that asks his mate to teach him how to be better. Without knowledge and intimacy, that is impossible. You share that type of information with the hope that he or /she is your forever story. You also do this with the notion that they'll reciprocate the same level of honesty and transparency. Therefore, it's easy to make love and not war.

It's easy to go through the ups and downs that life will throw you. Life WILL throw you ups and downs. Again, life will throw you ups and downs. But with the right level of intimacy, which grows into a beautiful relationship, you will be able to shout and dance on the mountaintops and truly persevere in the dark valleys. Because of this type of intimacy, you feel comfortable bringing new life into this world with that man or woman.

You have developed and created a world that never excludes them. And God forbid if they leave this earth before you. You quickly realize that you'll never find a relationship quite the same because you invested the time needed to learn and grow with that person. It won't be impossible to find another love like that. Don't get me wrong, love may come back around, but it will take a little more time. The cycle of intimacy just restarts. Good people, this is how your relationship with our Heavenly Father should be.

You cannot have faith if you don't know the person you're trusting and depending on. You must spend time with God. You must study Him. You must learn what He loves and what He hates. You must learn what pleases Him and what angers Him. Let's look at the disciples.

They were so in tune with Jesus that they began to pick up His ways, His words, His truth, and when He left the Holy Spirit on earth to indwell us, they were able to do, as He said, in John chapter 14 and 12...greater works.

> *"12 "Truly, truly, I say to you, whoever believes in me will also do the works that I do; and greater works than these will he do, because I am going to the Father."*

No work is higher than the cross, but because of it, we are charged on earth to carry the torch of Jesus Christ. And that requires us to know Him, His Word, and Holy Spirit so well that we, too, can perform greater works. Truth be truth, the Church hasn't been the same because we have lost real intimacy with the Father. Giftings didn't just stop after the disciples left this earth.

We must seek a sincere relationship with the Master, so He can empower us to continue to walk into our callings He designed for us. Healings can still take place, and miracles can even happen, salvation is still available. But if you don't know God, I mean really know God, how can we allow His Spirit to flow through us? How? There is no intimacy without relationship. I then subscribe to the thought that there is no faith without intimacy.

You should have a fervent spirit, and you should pay attention and continuously develop intimacy with God. Jesus is our most exceptional example, and He left Holy Spirit to dwell within us. By way of Holy Spirit, we come to learn the desires of the Father for our lives. God wants us to talk to Him about our childhoods, how we were hurt, and how we didn't understand why He allowed certain things to happen to us or our loved ones, which would ultimately shape our adult lives. He wants to know when we are sorry for making poor choices, and He desires for us to come to Him with hearts of repentance.

He wants to know that in Him, you truly live, move, and have your being. If you know me, you know that two of my favorite songs are by Dr. Charles Hayes', "Jesus can Work it Out" and Jason Nelson's "Nothing Without You." It's nothing short of fantastic when we shower God with the same types of accolades, thanks, and praise that we often give to the people who consider to be close to us. And if you don't brag on Him and how incredibly DOPE He is, start now! God wants to show you that He knew you first and He only wants the best for you.

He wants to show you what unconditional love looks like, the love we can never give as humans, although we try. It's impossible for us in our flesh tents to give unconditional anything. That type of love can only come from above. And get this, He wants to show you what the best kind of provision looks like, so that you will recognize the fakes and phonies a mile away. He disciplines and corrects like any great parent, but only because you have the purpose and destiny, He placed inside of you. Necessary is your assignment in His kingdom. Praise the Lord!

He can only share what He knows, what He owns, who He truly is, and how amazing He thinks you are if you let Him come inside. He will not, and trust me when I say this, He will <u>not</u> force Himself on you. There is a such thing as free will. Just because He is a just and fair God doesn't mean He is forceful. Our God wants to have an invitation from you.

He wants to know you intimately so that you can understand Him on levels you never knew were possible. He wants you to learn His heart in ways that you never thought existed. And if you think you'll learn everything in just a year, three years, or only five years, you will quickly realize that this is a lifetime of learning, loving, sharing, growing, pruning, and intimacy. HashtagRELATIONSHIP-GOALS.

The very first sermon I preached was about how your conditions don't determine your position. At the end of the message, I told the congregation about what God desired of us so that we could learn from every rough condition we found ourselves in. I spoke about what we needed to do to elevate to the next position, but before we rushed to the grand finale I asked them the same question I'll pose to you. It's quite simple. Here it goes.

How many of you keep your clothes on when you take a shower? Did you laugh like they did? I hope so, because not for nothing, you'd look ridiculous if you did. Do you know how heavy jeans are when they're wet? Do you know the amount of weight you would carry with wet clothes on in the shower? That question, in its original and now present design, is to demonstrate a straightforward point, you take a shower naked.

Therefore, that's how we should approach God. We should present ourselves naked and unashamed because that weight will soon become unbearable, uncomfortable, and even begin to smell if worn too long. While He knows all and sees all, He still enjoys a great time of intimacy. Being naked makes some of us uncomfortable; I used to be because I felt like I needed to lose a million pounds first, seriously. Being naked isn't always an easy thing to be.

That's why many won't do it. Instead, we go to another religion that makes us feel better by requiring less of us, one where a relationship isn't that important, one where showering with layers is cool. Let's imagine how many opportunities we've missed for a seed to be planted within us because we only wanted to come to God halfway undressed. I mean if you're into quickies that works, but where's the intimacy in that?

We need to trust Him entirely if He's impregnating us and allowing us to birth greatness, ideas, inventions, companies, churches, and more. There's nothing like being naked and free. I'm cool with that now, but it took some time. I encourage you to ask Holy Spirit for help if being vulnerable isn't your thing. Just whisper, "I want to be naked." I guarantee you Holy Spirit will not let you down, and Jesus will intercede like never before because He's excited to see us in love with His Father just like He is.

Without intimacy, there's no relationship. Without intimacy and relationship, there's no faith. I know firsthand that faith can and will rock your boat. Happy Sailing!

— ·· — ·· — ·

<u>Your Lifework:</u>

I know that it's not easy to get naked before the Lord. We feel free being naked around everyone else BUT the Father. We even share our intimate life details with our friends and never mention a word to God. How? Why? Most times it's just easier to talk to your friends. But we have to make being friends with God easy. We have to remember that intimacy with the Father is for a purpose. The largest one is the call on our lives.

Becoming intimate with God allows us to heal quicker from our pasts so that we can live in the present and future days free. Will we still experience periods of discomfort? ABSOLUTELY, but at least we have the bestest friend in the entire universe on our side. So, do me a favor, wait scratch that, do YOURSELF a favor, and start now.

Write down some areas you've never uttered with your mouth during your prayer times. After that, begin to speak about them with your Daddy. He is waiting, He is ready, and He is more than able to handle every weight you have to cast on Him. He loves you, son. He loves you, daughter. TRUST HIM.

4

Faith Rocked My Boat

DO YOU TRUST GOD, OR DON'T YOU?
SIMPLE QUESTION, RIGHT? SOME KNOW ME FROM THAT COMPLI-
CATED YET STRAIGHTFORWARD INQUIRY. I DIDN'T STUMBLE UPON IT. I
EITHER TRUST GOD, OR I DON'T. THERE IS NO IN-BETWEEN. AT TIMES
YOUR FAITH WILL BE TESTED, BUT DON'T WAVER. STAND FIRM ON THE
PROMISES OF THE LORD FOR YOUR LIFE. AFTER ALL,
SEEING IS BELIEVING, AND NOT SEEING IS FAITH.

I pray this is all making sense to you. I mean, faith is so important that sometimes it's impossible for me to not grow in it, or should I say I'm not sure I'm growing in it. Faith and faith ALONE is how we ended up moving to Texas. People ask us a million times a day, "Why in the entire world would you move to the country, and not only uproot your children's lives, but start a ministry?" We've asked ourselves the same question.

Who does that? No, for seriousness. Who says, "Hey...let's just leave everything God has allowed us to build and start over, no real security, no plan, but let's just do it." [Insert scream.] I often go back in my mind to see that my faith indeed grew in Christ. I've often subscribed to the Pastor Sone (my nickname) question of the day: "Do you trust God or don't you?"

That's typically where our conversation will end if you talk to me for an extended amount of time. We are certainly going to point to the importance of the cross, and then I'm going to ask you if you trust God or not, as you profess. I ask the question at every single counseling session and every single life coaching session with a believer. Even if you are just seeking general counsel, I will work that phrase into the mix. Let me paint yet another picture for you all.

We're going to rewind to the year 2016, which was the year of our great migration and happened to be my last year of seminary, our son's last year as a middle schooler, and our daughter's last year as an elementary student. We had three move-up days. You get it. Three. Whoa...the complete number! I will be honest with you. I just caught that revelation about the number three. Thank you, Lord!

Okay, I'm back. As a seminarian, I had to attend a personal retreat. You could take it any time during your college career, but most graduates and upperclassmen said that your final couple of semesters was the perfect time to go. The retreat was a time you spent alone with God, your thoughts, pen, and paper. NO DISTRACTIONS were allowed.

My tribe knows that I am a student of Bishop T. D. Jakes' teachings. I have several pastors that I follow and revere, but he and Lady Serita's leadership has blessed my life for many years and a myriad of reasons. I'd like to attribute my love for their ministry and his teachings to my husband's mother. We must've purchased every VHS and DVD set he has had ever made for her back in the day. In real life, she has to have boxes of those treasures.

I started paying more attention to Bishop Jakes when God began to tug on my heart in high school when being forced to watch those same VHS tapes we purchased. LOL! Husband's mother rarely watched anything else. So attending one of his conferences was inevitable. It was the perfect choice. However, because I am a true procrastinator (please pray for me, I'm about 70% delivered, maybe 68.9%), I waited until the end of March to pray about going to the conference that was less than a month away.

At that time, I was the minister of music at the Southern Baptist Church of Philadelphia, PA, under the leadership of Pastor Keith and Lady Bertina Pelzer. God bless the angels of the house (insider). LOL! No, but seriously, these two have been supportive of my family and me, so when I told him about attending Jakes' conference, he gave me his blessings, as I knew he would.

In my small mind, the International Pastors and Leadership Conference of 2016 (IP&L) was going to be the place where I'd gather as much information and resources for my pastor and the church. I was just a leader going to "grow." And with a theme like "Think Yourself CLEAR (Creative Leaders Emerge And Recharge)", I knew I was on the right path. I was an eMember of The Potter's House.

I joined in 2014 when a transition took place in our lives concerning our place of worship; this is when God initially began to challenge our faith. But I had to be there, and God made some significant ways for me to make it Orlando, FL. When I finally touched down, my mind was blown. Let's say that I had never experienced the Father in such a pure, unadulterated way.

Not only did I learn and gather the information that I ultimately would need for my current church, my faith catapulted. You don't understand. I grew in faith right before my very own eyes. Picture me, dressed in a flight suit and a helmet, like those old cartoons, and someone putting me in one of those cannons. Now, visualize someone lighting that little wick on the back and me shooting up into the sky somewhere. How funny is that? LOL!

I legit felt like my fervor, attentiveness, and intimacy all multiplied simultaneously and supernaturally. Although I had still failed in life at times, I no longer wanted to stay the same after that conference. It was like I was baptized, if you can see it, in a pool of faith. It supported my foundational mantra I gave to others often, trusting God or not trusting Him. The conclusion I drew was simple. I TRUSTED God!

I trusted Him to help me to sin, less. I trusted Him to keep me focused. I trusted Him with all of my finances, every single area of them. I trusted Him with broken relationships. I trusted Him with levels of my unforgiveness. I trusted Him with ALL of me FOR REAL this time. Like real-life kind of trust.

I repented for the areas of doubt and the periods when I was supposed to act, but stood still. I promised that no matter what the enemy would throw my way, I'd have faith. I was IN THE BOAT. I resembled the kid in the classroom who did all of their homework, yes finally, and darn near jumped out of their chair from raising their hand to give the *correct* answer.

I'm cracking up and getting hype as I recall when I was drenched, soaked, and dripping in faith. I vividly recall screaming at the top of my lungs at one point during worship, "TRUST ME!" Now you know that's just like asking for patience, right? Who does that, and why? I've been there and done that before, and maybe God needs to instruct Holy Spirit to offer the inspiration for another book about that journey. I've never asked for patience again, but I was now in trouble with this whole "trust me" situation.

I was taking my walk seriously now at the young age of 36 and a ½. God had somehow made heaven and earth move for me even to be there, so if I didn't rededicate my whole existence, I would've been crazy, especially at that moment. There is a such thing as divine timing and appointments. I wasn't missing mine. I was on a high that can never be reached via man-made substances. No challenge could shake or move me, no blow to the head or chin was gonna take me out this time.

I believed and was okay with not seeing what was ahead of me. Thank you, Jesus! So, when I got home, Husband said, "How was the experience? Are you still on fire? And I exclaimed, "OF COURSE!" I began telling him about the sessions, the messages, the encounter, and the many feelings that met me at IP&L 2016. Husband then said that he was glad that I had so much faith, as he slid a letter from our landlord to me that said, in a nutshell, "You ain't gotta leave PA, but you gotta get outta here by May 31st."

I busted out laughing, literally cracking up. I remember being so hype about what was next because the entire time, in my heart and mind, I was still in the boat, but I was now approaching my "walk on the water moment." I was like, "Let's do this!" We did what we had to do and packed up everything we owned, kids, and pets, all right at the end of a school year, which was still in progress. Ordinarily, this pill would be a shameful one to swallow...having to leave with nowhere to go, but we took it in stride and moved in with my mother-in-love.

I remember how Husband and I even stayed in the house, without permission, after packing and sending the kids to his mother's house because we couldn't believe we had no place to go. We would travel back and forth between work, the old house, and his mom's house while looking for rentals with no luck. How does that happen? NO houses or even apartments available? Do you know how large Philadelphia is? We would also get a hotel room, here and there, to keep us off the floor of the house. It was an experience. Correction...it was *our* experience.

We couldn't believe that nobody had a place for us to rent. It was eerily weird. Before our brief stint of homelessness, we confided in a couple we knew for some time, the Throwers, about our current housing crisis. (Rest in peace Unc) From that conversation, a word from the Lord came, and Killeen, Texas, was mentioned. Now since I was still on this faith cloud, I was like okay, Texas, it is!

I guess my longtime desire to move to Georgia was now off the table because God said Texas. I felt it in my spirit. Husband's reaction to the word given was far from ecstatic. I will leave that right there. So from IP&L, which was April 21st-23rd, to the word we received when I got home, to us realizing that May 31st was quickly approaching, we had to make a decision. Do we trust God, or don't we? And as you can surmise, we did. Texas it was, but know that the "yes" came with Husband asking God for some ridiculous things or as we religious folk say...signs that this was Him speaking. I seriously thought God was about to smite my new-found bold faith because of Husband's requests. The man I married asked God to show him a million things.

He wanted to see a license plate from Texas that had to be on an actual moving vehicle, and that was just one of his insane requests. It was horrible. But get this, God delivered affirmation after affirmation. Unbelievable. I must admit that even with my faith on a trillion, Husband and I concluded that God meant to relocate us to Austin and not Killeen. I mean, it fit us better. Judge somebody else.

We have all been there when God is specific but somehow we twist it to have a totally new meaning. We twist it to something we thought He meant, but it really was what we wanted all along. You know it wasn't just us doing that. LOL! But let me explain why we felt that way. Some eight years ago, we visited Killeen.

Our group, 1Prayz Ministries, who happens to have a single on all musical outlets right now, "My Joy," which can be purchased TODAY, ministered there. We sang at Excellent Covenant Power-house Ministries for Pastors Kelvin and Sabrina Nero's anniversary services. One of my friends and her family moved to a surrounding city a couple of years prior.

She had been trying to get us to move to Texas, but I was like, there wasn't a chance in the world. I can recall Husband and I laughing about how we'd never live in Killeen. Like NEVER! EVER! NEVER! Yeah, I think that's how it went. So here we were back in July 2016. My vacation was quickly approaching, and we had decided to drive to Austin to secure a place to live, jobs, and to get acclimated to our new surroundings.

So, about that boat. I was *on* it. I was legit asking Jesus to tag me. And just like that, I was walking on water, but then I went with the whole not living in Killeen idea; I was much like Peter. I began to sink. Yeah, totally on a one-way ride to the bottom. LOL! But let me take some time to give you the details about the "boat experience."

You need to have the entire scriptural reference for proper context. Matthew 14:22-30 reads:

> "*22 Immediately he made the disciples get into the boat and go before him to the other side, while he dismissed the crowds. 23 And after he had dismissed the crowds, he went up on the mountain by himself to pray. When evening came, he was there alone, 24 but the boat by this time was a long way from the land, beaten by the waves, for the wind was against them. 25 And in the fourth watch of the night he came to them, walking on the sea. 26 But when the disciples saw him walking on the sea, they were terrified, and said, "It is a ghost!" and they cried out in fear. 27 But immediately Jesus spoke to them, saying, "Take heart; it is I. Do not be afraid." 28 And Peter answered him, "Lord, if it is you, command me to come to you on the water." 29 He said, "Come." So Peter got out of the boat and walked on the water and came to Jesus. 30 But when he saw the wind, he was afraid, and beginning to sink he cried out, "Lord, save me."*

During our lapse in judgment, okay straight disobedience, we enjoyed Austin. We thought we were supposed to move there. We had a full itinerary y'all. We were driving from Philly to Austin, from Austin to State College because I had to preach at an event at our college church, and then back to Philly. Besides doing the most with the absolute least, I want to be crystal clear.

While you are trying to trust God with all your might, there may come a time when you become distracted and begin to sink, but because God is full of grace and mercy, he will still provide a way out for you. Jesus will always intercede because He knows we are hardheaded at times, wrapped up in these flesh tents, and Holy Spirit will still indwell. It's during these times of potentially dangerous "brain farts" that a way of escape appears almost instantly.

Listen, stay strong in your faith, even if it feels strange or new. God knows best. Can I just testify? While on the road to the wrong location, I got an email from my job asking me to stay with the company. That was on Friday when we left. On the road, I opened my email, and they said they created an entirely new remote position. So on day ONE of us hitting the road to Austin, and NOT Killeen, God had already prepared the financial provision. Go ahead, shout with me!

Not knowing that the Lord was solving an issue and trying to get our attention, our happiness did not deter us from spending time in Austin to find housing, since we didn't have to worry about me finding a job. Now the job hunt was split in half. Husband just needed his gig. The Lord never ceases to amaze me!

He told me when we said yes to the move that no *person* would get any credit, because all the glory belonged to Him. I'm sure He and Elisha were laughing at me because I had missed it. What did I miss? Wait for it.

So we finally got to Austin, and house shopping was in full effect with our realtor.

Yes, we had a whole realtor. LOL! She was such a fantastic agent too. She kept the houses within our budget and was extremely knowledgeable about the area. She was an older woman who loved God and wasn't ashamed to tell it, so we felt right at home. She almost killed us with her driving, but praise God we are here to tell the story.

We had completed the applications we needed to complete for the houses we loved, found leads on a job for Husband, enjoyed sightseeing and ate all the banging food in Austin, and then hit the road to State College, PA. Now you know whenever you start following God's will for your life for seriousness, you will be met with challenges that just seem random, right? As we approached PA, we got a flat tire. We had driven clear across the world with not even a hiccup.

Well, wait, we did break down in Tennessee when we stopped to visit our little sister. I forgot about that one. LOL! The radio's fuse had blown, and honestly, I believe both instances were a test for Husband. God wanted to see if he was going to be like, "NOPE! NO TEXAS!"

He did handle each instance with "his style" of patience, though. If you know him personally, you know what "his style" means too. I'm chuckling because I can just hear him now. But just like Papa John's son, he got us back on the road in one piece, and we got to State College safely. God moved awesomely at the service.

You wouldn't believe that their theme was surrounding the "YES" we give God. My message was about surrendering to God. I cannot make this up. So after God had His way and we fellowshipped with our State College family, we headed back home to await the news that was forthcoming about our new place in Austin.

Let's take a look at the calendar that hung in my office at work. **I believe seeing is believing and not seeing is faith.** Ha! I love the little drawings, my daughter, better known as Pretty Gyrl, wrote when she visited me. I took a picture of the calendar to keep her words of encouragement. She's truly a sweetheart.

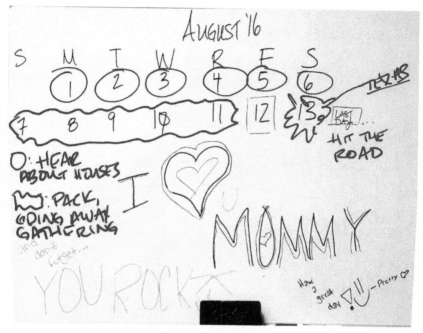

As you can see, time was of the essence. Vacation and traveling ended on July 24th, 2016. The realtor said we'd hear back quickly, and on July 27th, I got the first of many disappointing calls. I mean, Austin delivered blow after blow. Every single house, townhouse, and apartment owner said "no" to us. If you were unaware, Texas is its own country, hence the name Lone Star state.

They didn't like the idea of the kids and I moving without my husband. We were going down first to start the registration process for school and get settled until he finished up at his old job. One property manager said, "Is this a child support thing?" I told her no and explained our situation. She respectfully sent me an email letting me know that the owner of the house wanted the entire family in Texas, not just part of us. Oh joy!

Our sister-in-love, Leslie, said, "John (Juan's brother aka Wesely) and I wanted to throw you a send-off get-together." She had no clue that we did NOT have a place to live yet. We were now here:

The faith I lost, but for a moment, when I began to sink, suddenly began to rise within me. It made me feel like I had another chance. Matthew 14:30-33 reads:

"30 But when he saw the wind, he was afraid, and beginning to sink he cried out, "Lord, save me." 31 Jesus immediately reached out his hand and took hold of him, saying to him, "O you of little faith, why did you doubt?" 32 And when they got into the boat, the wind ceased. 33 And those in the boat worshiped him, saying, "Truly you are the Son of God."

As the scripture says, when Peter realized that he was walking on water, his surroundings began to distract him, and he began to sink, but he cried out to the Lord while he was doing so. I love that he cried. When you cry, you are vulnerable. There's that word, immediately, again.

When men cry today, society can make them believe they're weak or not masculine enough, but the contrary is right in this story. Peter knew that his emotions were of no importance; he was safe. So safe that he could cry. I imagine it was a cry of desperation too. I don't know about you, but if I thought I was drowning, I'd be crying, flailing my arms, kicking, and then yelling would soon follow.

When Jesus heard Peter's cry, He IMMEDIATELY reached His hand out. He reprimanded him with love and He gave a gentle and soothing comment of encouragement. How many times has God IMMEDIATELY stepped in on your behalf? With no questions? I took it as Jesus merely stating the obvious, "Do you trust me, or don't you?"

And how can you not worship and praise a God as dope as that? I also love to point out that sometimes others just need to see you leave the boat. Us relocating was not necessarily about Juan, Sonya, Vidal, Reid, and our dogs Rhema and Eden (and now Philly Mae).

It was about God getting all of the glory because even in our weakness, He proved that He was a protector and a promise keeper.

For those who are always looking to get that invite onto the water, praise and worship our Lord right now. Put the book or tablet down, or if you're listening, take the headphones off and worship Him! He will keep you when you take your shaky-knees walk onto the water. Turn to your neighbor and say, "Git outta da boat!" That was for my country folk.

The bottom line is that there will be people who want to receive a tag, and there will be those who are onlookers. Neither stance is higher than the other, but they each produce a different result. The goal, is to desire that "tag you're it" type of nudge. Even if you begin to sink, you have to trust that Jesus' hand of rescue will be there IMMEDIATELY. So we were uber focused at this point.

Now that we had a fresh dip in the water, we were ready to fight on, and Jesus didn't even yell at us for taking His intercession for granted. He did what He always does and lent us His hand. My faith was now official   back on 10,000,000,000, and if you caught it, I said, "we," not just "I." Husband was on board. My boat experience wasn't just for me. Ayyyyyyyyyyyye!

We were fast approaching the first day of the weekend in August, the month we were moving. On Friday, August 5th, 2016, at approximately 10 a.m., I sat in my office at what is now my previous place of employment and said, "God, I'm sorry. If it's Your will for us to live in Killeen, I will obey You completely."

Notice I said *previous* place of employment. God knew the expiration date of that too. Let's chat about that at my class, coming to your area soon. There's just too many life lessons to squeeze in one book. We'd all be crying and shouting and all of that before I could get another sentence out. LOL! Now, we're here:

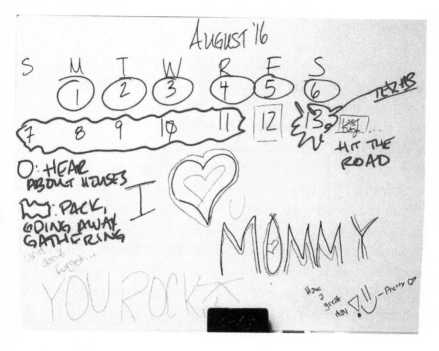

I recall sitting in my office, crying at my desk, trying to figure out what was next. We told the whole world that our send-off was on August 10th, 2016, and we were out for good that Friday, the 12th. We even encouraged love offerings because if we're honest, we would have never made it to Texas without all of the help and outpouring of love we were blessed with, financially . The blessings were beyond our wildest imagination. We wanted for nothing on the road. #GratefulAlways

But before I finish this office story, let me fast-forward a little to the night of the party. I have a scene from the highlight reel; there were so many. Besides the fact that we were taken aback by big brosef and big sis wanting to host such an event, we had such a memorable time. Like, get this, the FranklinFam drove 6 hours roundtrip to say, "We love you, and we will miss you," and to bless us financially.

They only spent about half an hour with our guests and us before they had to hit the road. We were SO blown away by this gesture of love! Do people like this exist anymore? Yep...they do, and they're our family. Wendell and Kikora Franklin are gems that have been in our lives for over 14 years.

I remember us meeting when KiKi was pregnant with her son Gyasi, and I was pregnant with Pretty Gyrl (her birth name is Reid, but she is sooooo pretty). They're weeks apart. These two and their beautiful children (Khari and Lila too) are a blessing, and I don't think we ever really said thank you, so I'm saying it right here, THANK YOU!!! You guys don't even know how special we felt for that genuine display of love.

Okay, now back to me balling at my desk at work on August 5th, an exact week from us preparing to leave. After my plea and moment of repentance, I started searching for houses in the city of Killeen. I'd come across many, but there was one that stood out. It was the right price point, it was in an area where the schools weren't horrible, and the pictures were terrific.

Now let me remind you of one minor fact, we never looked for places to live in Killeen while visiting Texas in July. We spent our entire week in Austin. So not only was I finally dried off from this boat ride, now I'm blindfolded. They don't call me crazy for nothing. I didn't even call to wake Husband up. He was resting before heading to work later that night.

I went on ahead and said, "We'll take it," put in the application, and moved on with my day. At this point, I was just all in my faith. The workday came to an end, and aside from the property manager calling me to verify that he received everything, I didn't hear anything else about the house. I picked up Pretty and Buddy from school and headed to my mom-in-love's house, where every day felt like we were on trial.

My mom had too many questions and opinions, and my mom-in-love had not stopped saying how she just didn't understand how we were packing up the kids to go to Texas with no house yet. LOL! Hindsight is 20/20, praise God, and I get why they were so vocal and legitimately concerned. Parents will always desire the best for their children, and they prefer that our lives have the least amount of struggle. We feel the same way about our kids. But we wanted our mothers to know that the same God they taught us to know and love had our backs, fronts, sides, and everything in between.

While there were still unknowns, the largest one being where we'd lay our heads, our beautiful mothers took on all the worry for us. After a brief interrogation, I went to the basement to take a quick nap with Pretty Gyrl. Not only was this process draining, but I like naps. It's part of my life's routine, so judge someone else. I promise you that taking a nap every day extends your life by...I'm not sure, but there has to be a fact out there that proves my theory!

Once we woke up, Pretty was ready to eat, and so was Buddy. We didn't get to see Husband before he headed to work since he had a longer drive to get to work, now that we were in Philly. I never filled him in about the happenings of the day...mainly the fact that I just applied to live somewhere without asking him to review the house. There was no way to explain a feeling of not knowing where you're going to live in a brand new state. I had to act swiftly. I wouldn't do that ordinarily, but the way my faith was, I had to trust that God had it.

As I headed upstairs to cook dinner, I didn't even think about the fact that I hadn't heard back from the property manager. I mean, I did place our entire living situation in his hands. And yes, we alllllllllll know that God is in control, but I'm just saying. I realized I had left my phone at the door in my bag. And since we cannot live without our phones, I went to see what I missed. There was only one missed call and one voicemail, confirming that I was not as popular as all would believe. LOL! The number was a 512 area code, which is Austin, so I immediately got into my feelings. I was like, oh so noooooow y'all wanna call me in Austin?!

Instantly, the downward spiral began in my mind. If you recall, I couldn't include Husband on the application in Austin because most of the properties wanted us to move together. So the Killeen application was just in my name along with the kids. It only had my credit on it, which at times, as Husband put it, resembled the time after school specials used to come on. LOL! I was sweating in my boots and hadn't even checked the message yet.

I knew I didn't make as much money as my education and experience dictated, so applying for anything that depended on credit was just nerve-racking. Creditworthiness was one of the reasons why I had stopped talking to my mother about the move. She had insisted that we stay another year to build up our credit scores, but I was like, "NO! God said, "GO"!" Now back to this mysterious phone call. I finally clicked play on the voicemail icon, and a man's voice said, "Mrs. Sessoms, I just wanted to call to say, congratulations, and welcome to Texas! I'll be emailing you yadda, yadda, yadda, and yadda."

I went downstairs and ran in that basement, shouting and screaming. I'm pretty sure there was an ugly cry too, snot and all. I then called Husband, which I never did, while he was at work. He was an armed security officer in a power plant, and he carried loaded weapons and kind of needed to be alert at all times. At his job, he was prohibited from using the phone until his break. The reception was horrible too, so a call rarely got through. This was important, though, so I took a risk and called anyway. Would you believe I got through, and he picked up?!

He quickly reminded me that he had but a few seconds because he couldn't talk at work, but wanted to check to be sure we were okay. I hurriedly exclaimed, "We got the house!!" I started describing the one God chose for us, and he then said, "The one I emailed you about?" To myself, I was like, "Is he trying to take credit for the communing me and Jesus had in my office?" LOL! I didn't consult him before I applied, so he had no clue the house was even a choice. He was hype too, but had to get back to work.

Once he got off we began to rejoice together. We realized that his email never got through to me, EVER. He selected the same house and two other homes in Killeen. Do you see how the Lord kept us knitted together? Finally, a week before leaving, I could show our mothers where we'd be living since they drove us nuts the most. Thank you, JESUS! But it wouldn't be a story of faith if it were that easy. Don't forget that we signed a lease, sent money for our deposit and first month's rent, and hadn't even seen the place in person. Talk about blind faith.

I have to say thanks to our realtor because even though she didn't carry a license for the Killeen area, she was still able to take my friend, who lived in Texas, to the house to look around. So I not only had to trust God, but I had to believe that my friend would know what was best. I appreciate both of them for going to see the place, but their reviews were like... "it's an okay starter house." LOL! The money was gone, and my faith was now on 20,000,000,000, no matter what.

I mean, we didn't even survey this land. We were presented with yet another boat moment all over again. Although we didn't get the news we wanted to hear at first, and got our boat rocked, we paid attention, used the correct instructions, and didn't sink this time. I was staying on the boat this time but was still HYPE to begin the new journey. The lesson from these boat experiences was that I needed to be tenacious.

What does tenacity mean? It's defined as "the quality or fact of being able to grip something firmly; grip; the quality or fact of being very determined; determination; the quality or fact of continuing to exist; persistence." Did you get all of that? I hope you saw that I was persistent in my pursuit to see God move on our behalf no matter what.

I ran the race set before me and am still running with endurance that only the Father can give. It's the type of determination we see displayed in the woman with the issue of blood. This story appears in

Mark 5:25-34, Matthew 9:20-22, and Luke 8:43-48. Let's look at Luke's account:

"⁴³And there was a woman who had had a discharge of blood for twelve years, and though she had spent all her living on physicians, she could not be healed by anyone. ⁴⁴She came up behind him and touched the fringe of his garment, and immediately her discharge of blood ceased. ⁴⁵And Jesus said, "Who was it that touched me?" When all denied it, Peter said, "Master, the crowds surround you and are pressing in on you!" ⁴⁶But Jesus said, "Someone touched me, for I perceive that power has gone out from me." ⁴⁷And when the woman saw that she was not hidden, she came trembling, and falling down before him declared in the presence of all the people why she had touched him, and how she had been immediately healed. ⁴⁸And he said to her, "Daughter, your faith has made you well; go in peace."

Many important things are going on at once in this story. If you're ever in Killeen, join us at the Sound Of Worship Center, I hear the pastor there is incredible. Yes. I gave my ministry a shameless plug. But listen, this woman had to stay away from civilization for 12 entire years. She was ostracized. Her treatment in society was equivalent to that of a leper. Who in the world bleeds for 12 years?!I admire this woman's tenacity. She was NOT leaving without being healed.

Are you that bold with your life? With the gifts God placed inside of you? With your responsibilities? Are you brave enough to crawl on the ground, probably getting trampled, not caring about being embarrassed yet again, to touch the fringe of Jesus' garment? A fringe? His outfit had tiny strings of fabric hanging from it, and she believed that if she could just get to that small piece of material, her problem would be solved. Are you tenacious like this? The text says that this woman touched those tiny strings, and IMMEDIATELY she got her healing.

Here's that word *immediately* again. When Peter was sinking in the water, and he cried out for help, Jesus *immediately* rescued him. This young woman with the issue of blood was *immediately* healed after coming in contact with the Son of God. When Jesus asked who touched him, Peter, go figure, was the guy with all the sarcasm. Who talks that way to the Savior of the entire world?

That's how I know that me and Peter would get along. He straight told Jesus that he had no clue who touched him since there were like thousands of people around. He was accurate in his assessment of the surroundings, but Jesus felt that some power left Him. You mean to tell me that if I'm tenacious enough to get on my knees and crawl, all scraped up, coming just as I am, right where I am, just to touch a tiny piece of Jesus' garment, I can be made whole? Wait, and Jesus will know that it wasn't His body, but His clothes that I touched?

Even His garments are full of the anointing, my God. That's amazing! We also can't help but wonder if the woman was trying to run away once Jesus realized someone had touched Him. If you allow me to use my imagination for a quick second, we know that she was on the ground or close to it because she touched the fringe, the hem, the border of his garment. We also know that in verse 47, it says that she was trembling.

I gather she was excited, relieved, and overwhelmed. She had her healing! I can see the crowd almost splitting in two when Jesus asked who touched Him, uncovering her as she was trying to scurry away. I can visualize the moment when she realized everyone was looking at her, which left her with no choice but to come back and fall before Jesus. Don't miss the big "ah-ha" moment. The Bible says that she realized she wasn't hidden any longer, so she came back. She tried to get out of dodge. That's how we are sometimes.

We ask the Lord to heal us, to bless us, to deliver us, to impart in us, and when He does, we're out, like "Thanks for the gumball, Mickey!" We are a trip! For an entire lifetime we've been plagued, God delivers us, and we don't even give Him thanks. Shameful! I honestly believe, however, that this woman was so nervous that she thought she'd rrrrrrrrrreally get in trouble since she was already a known outcast. After she runs back to the scene of her healing and falls before Jesus to admit it was her who touched Him, why she did it, and how she stopped bleeding, I can see Jesus cutting her off, mid-explanation.

She was probably breathing all heavy trying to talk, and as soon as she started to give her speech, He politely signaled to her to hush and told her that her faith made her well. NOW STOP right here!!! Do you mean that Jesus' garments did not carry the anointing? They didn't glow or possess healing power? Uhhhhhhhh no!

She believed that she could receive healing, which seemed impossible, and placed her trust in the man who made all things possible. Her FAITH made her whole. I also love how Jesus made a public declaration. He gave her a "get out jail free" card. Now everyone in the city would know that Jesus co-signed on her tenacious and driven self. That silenced any opportunities for folks to make fun of her.

Jesus declared not only that she had received her healing, but also that she possessed faith, something He was trying to educate everyone about anyway. It's the same faith we need to grab hold of today. And not faith so that we can get things, but faith so that we can gain healing. True healing. We can pick this story apart, I'm sure and get into theological debates, but I selected it to show that having tenacity is necessary for this journey called life.

In other words, I need to have a fervor about me, I need to be sure to pay attention at all times so I don't miss a directive, I need to work on my intimacy with God which leads to a deeper relationship, and I need to stay tenacious. Look, you have a life to lead with many more obstacles and challenges that will *face you*, not obstacles and challenges that *you* will face. Sometimes you have no clue that trouble is looking for you. Pat yourself on the back for knowing these things in advance.

If there is one thing that stuck with me throughout this experience, it is the pressing notion that faith ain't over.

— ·· — ·· — ·

Your Lifework:

What a journey! Prayerfully, as you work on your lifework, you feel encouraged knowing that faith is possible for you too.

The real question now is simple, beyond if you trust God or not, and it's this: How bad do you want it? And your "it" can be healing, it can be your prophecies that you would like fulfilled in your life, it can be a better relationship with your parents, your spouse, it can be the directive for your purpose, instructions on how to bring your destiny to fruition. Only you know what "it" is. Only you know why "it" is. Only you know how "it" is. Only you know where "it" is. And because of that, only you can chase after "it." CRAWL!!! Push through the crowds! CRAWL!!! Get to where "it" is! CRAWL!!!

Write it down. What are you expecting from God? What instructions is He giving you to accomplish those things? Write, write, write!

5

Faith Ain't Over

"My hope is built in nothing less than Jesus' blood and
righteousness. I dare not trust the sweetest frame, but
wholly trust in Jesus' name."
– Edward Mote, 1834

"YOU PROBABLY SANG THIS HYMN AS A YOUNGSTER, BUT WHERE DOES YOUR HOPE LIE TODAY? FAITH IS NOT HOPE. HOPING IS HAVING A MINDSET THAT IS OPTIMISTIC ABOUT WHAT YOU ARE EXPECTING. BE SURE TO PUT YOUR CONFIDENCE IN THE MAN WHO HASN'T LOST A BATTLE YET!"

It's now time to hit the road to Killeen, Texas! I have to say thank you to a previous co-worker for keeping our dog, Eden, for seven months until we could come back for her. And a special shout-out to Jeff and Shameeka for adopting our dog Jordan. We believe that Jordan was the estrogen needed in the house for you all to have that beautiful baby girl. I'm just saying...you're welcome. All jokes, but we are blessed to have had you guys caring for our dogs.

Now let's get back to the road. Still living out of bags and boxes, it was pretty easy to get all packed. We put everything we could into our cars and left enough room for my mother and us. I laugh when I think about it. My mom said she wanted to see where her baby was going to be living, and she supposedly was there to help us drive. Yeah, right, Lady (my mom's nickname that only I can call her). I swear she drove about three hours. Lady will tell you that she drove more hours than that, but don't you believe it! I have pictures of her knocked out.

Are you getting this visual of us packed to the brim in two vehicles? I pray you're having as much fun as I am, as I recall our faith journey. So far, we've seen a fervent spirit in action, learned how paying attention is mandatory for progress, concluded that intimacy is not just about sex, and recognized that being a tenacious individual is necessary in our daily walk with Christ. I started this book by making references to my childhood years, high school days, and then BOOM, I'm married with children and dogs.

But this is where I believe I can insert another stage of life—my college years. Sooooo much to say, sooooo little time. Prayerfully what I can summarize will suffice. This book is not about life lessons, sin, forgiveness, and all of that, because, if it were, we'd be here forever. In college, I went through a myriad of transitions that involved all of those things mentioned above. After graduating from Girls' High, I started my post-secondary career at the Ogontz cam-pus of The Pennsylvania State University.

When they decided to make Ogontz a four-year college, they changed its name to Penn State Abington, but for nostalgia's sake, we'll still call it Ogontz. Shout out to all my homies and homettes! 1997 marked the year I made it through an impressive four years of high school, and now college was knocking on my door. Elation overtook me as I was about to step into partial adulthood since I still lived at home.

I also knew there was still a call on my life because I felt it deep in my soul. I knew that God wanted more from me, but I wasn't ready to step into the light just yet. He started calling me in my junior year of Girls' High, I respectfully resisted, and since I was still alive, I figured I might as well keep the party going. After all, it was college. LOL! Ogontz was my opportunity to right some wrongs.

I learned how to be a better friend; my eyes became open to what I would look like in the "real" world, and I discovered what career I'd be drawn to, and so much more. You will hear and come to learn that college is the place where you find yourself, as if for your entire life until then, you were somehow lost. The saying is true; at least it was for me. As I stepped foot on the campus, I linked up with some folks that I love dearly to this very day.

I realized, too, that sinning was okay just as long as I re-pented...wait, what chapter was that? Yep, I fell into that lukewarm lifestyle real quick. I did whatever I wanted because I was "grown" now. I was driving, working, getting good grades, partying, and yadda yadda. But God was still faithful and kept me despite me. I KNOW somebody has that exact testimony...it can't just be me. Give me a little head nod so nobody can see. LOL!

Welcome to the chronicles of an Ogontz campus student. God sent me Jose Rodriguez, the Director of Minority Affairs at the time, and Dr. Valeria G. Harvell, who didn't even have her Ph.D. back then. She was, and still is, a dynamic professor who teaches African and African American Studies. She taught us everything about being Black. "Amazing" isn't even the word to describe her. Let's talk about these two awesome blessings that came from God Himself.

Jose was my first up-close-and-personal experience with a gay man, who was comfortable in his identity. He always repped his Latin roots. He also always talked about God loving us all and the necessity for diversity to be discussed everywhere. Jose stood by the fact that we were a colorful bunch of college students who would be responsible for running the country someday and raising children who would need to receive education in the same fashion.

He embraced me with my wannabe Latina self at that time, and he loved me so much that I didn't even focus on what our society spewed about his "type" of people. Honestly, why did society's opinions matter??? In the late '90s, being open about your sexuality was becoming popular. You see, I grew up living a semi-sheltered life until I entered high school and had friends exploring their sexual options, but remember, I went to an all-girls school.

This man in all of his greatness taught me how to love...period. Some would then say things like: "As believers, we don't agree with the homosexual lifestyle, so let's only hang out with folks who are not." Let's isolate, criticize, and demonize. Yep, that's Biblical. No, it's not. But at the culmination of my laughter came an observation. I would ask said narrow-minded individuals, "I thought we didn't agree with fornication, adultery, lying, stealing, and cheating either."

So how did we find ourselves married with boyfriends and girl-friends, how did we uncover lies and deceit among the leaders, how come the minister of music can still sing even though he's sleeping with the alto section, yes, the entire section?" I didn't get it back then. I would also like to add that this book isn't about what we're going to pick and choose to be "okay" with as believers. Nor is this a book that will debate topics that only God will ultimately judge. Yeah, this isn't that book.

So I'm going to leave this here – I learned how to love and accept everyone, no matter their shape, color, sex, religion, sexual preference, and all of that, after having a close and intimate relationship with Jose. I was a young Black woman who didn't speak a lick of Spanish, but he always invited me to every single function he had. He and Husband (who I was just dating back then...we got married in September of 2000) would even cut up all day every time they saw one another. God met me where I was, in all of my sin that I hid so very well, to teach me a lesson on real acceptance and love.

I was a horrible person, morally, when I began college. I was full of lust, I was selfish, I was self-centered, and I enjoyed all of it. I made choices and decisions that always came with severe consequences, like most bad choices typically do. Every seed sewn, be it a good seed or bad seed, reaps a harvest. Galatians 6:7-9 says:

> *"7Do not be deceived: God is not mocked, for whatever one sows, that will he also reap. 8For the one who sows to his own flesh will from the flesh reap corruption, but the one who sows to the Spirit will from the Spirit reap eternal life. 9And let us not grow weary of doing good, for in due season we will reap, if we do not give up."*

If it's planted and watered, it will grow, and you will reap. Some seeds grow slower than others, unfortunately. I didn't lose focus on Jose's love towards me and mine towards him. Our relationship didn't stand on a biblical debate on how he chose to live his life. He never judged me for my hidden sins, and I never sentenced him for his not-so-hidden lifestyle. I am so grateful for him, and I miss him dearly. I love you, Jose! Thank you so much!

Then, enters Dr. Valeria Gomez Harvell, the woman I wanted to become when I decided to live right. LOL! I grew so much, and if you have never encountered this Presbyterian Pastor who married a white man, and taught Black power like nobody's business, then you have not lived. I remember when everyone found out that Steve was a white man. How can you be "woke" and marry outside of your race? She said she didn't know about all of that, but Steve held her down and stood with her on those picket lines, fighting for racial equality, and she loved his mind. Two great people, I tell you.

I didn't know that I'd embrace the beauty in my Blackness like that in college either. I was so used to hanging with my Latin family that I hadn't dived into my culture much. I would often be shocked at some of the things she'd talk about too. She was good for telling us that "the man" was NOT gonna keep us down. I wanted her power, strength, strong sense of self-identity, individuality, and freedom; I mean, she would rock dashikis and thee most authentic afro ever.

When she came to our send-off she was still as beautiful as ever. Her presence carried the weight of royalty, just like when she walked into class late with her coffee and Reading Study Guides, aka RSGs in her hand. I didn't learn about her life on day one, of course. We had an intimate relationship. She invested her time in cultivating me. I sincerely desired so much to be her, I mean, I was and still am her favorite. YES, you heard it here first. I am Dr. Harvell's favorite student.

So to all her past, present, and future students – don't even think about claiming my sister/mentor. There will never be another "Reid." LOL! She would call us by our last names, like we were in the military. Yes, Reid is my maiden name, and we named our daughter the same thing.

I asked her questions about her parents, her upbringing, her life outside of teaching. I stayed after class to be around her more. I would even change my schedule to ensure I took at least one of her courses a semester. After leaving any conversation with her, I was excited about being a young Black woman, on my way to success. People say that you shouldn't be the smartest one in your circle. They also say that you should surround yourself with people representing where you'd like to be in life. I found my person, I found her.

So instead of hanging with my Latin crew and wishing I could speak Spanish to "fit in," I became more excited about my uniqueness: my beautiful Black self. They loved me still. But Dr. Harvell would give me books as gifts. That furthered my appreciation of my culture and my people's struggle, and I wanted to incite a revolution for any persons viewed as "problems" in our society. I needed to grasp this knowledge and spend this time with someone who knew more than me because I'd someday be raising beautiful brown babies of my own in a world that would unfortunately worsen.

I wanted Husband to now stand with me on picket lines like Steve did so we could fight social injustices. Yeah, college is real, folks. You go through a variety of motions and emotions. Dr. Harvell and I spent a lot of time together. We'd camp out in her office or chat it up on the phone. Through these exchanges, I became privy to a not-so-known fact; she was also a Pastor. [Inserts gasp and a quick run, because God has jokes.] I was like what?!

Now it all began to make sense. She would often refer to my "light," and here I was working on sinning more than ever to resist the tug on my heart. So now, my mentor is a beautiful, intelligent Black Queen who follows the Lord...great. LOL! I kindly told God that I saw what He was trying to do, but the world was still my playground, and I hopped on those swings the devil's camp set up for me and kicked my feet in the air like I didn't care. A whole mess! Even still, Dr. Harvell made such an impact on my life. My love for her won't ever fade. I am always grateful.

Now in year two of my newly found adulthoodedness, I had to choose my major and apply to Penn State's main campus. Yes, you had to apply if you began your career on a commonwealth campus. My sophomore year was also the year that I'd leave comfortability. The year my mother's only child had to make some life-impacting choices. It was time to depart from the nest and move into my first apartment, three hours away.

For those of you who have a hard time with the years and timelines, let me throw you a quick assist. I started high school in 1993 and graduated in 1997. My freshman year of college was from 1997 to 1998, and this second year was from 1998 to 1999...the year we all partied! Oh, and let's not forget that by the time you hit your sophomore year, you should already know better. Seriously, why in the world are you acting like you don't have a whole college career on the line?

You also are granted with many second chances. Your actual major and all of its classes don't start until you're a junior. You're still enjoying that prerequisite life of basic math, speech comm, biology, and all those other gen-ed courses you need to graduate. But prayerfully, you are on a quest to correct all your wrongs from your freshman year. Some of which include all of the horrible decisions and choices you made, whether knowingly or while aloof. Sophomore year is the year of redemption.

In comprehending what season of life I was in, I came to Jesus and decided to move a little differently but still stay in my quiet and hidden sin...the worst kind. Not only did I have Jose and Dr. Harvell trying to keep me on the straight and narrow, I had the honor to meet Robert Outterbridge. I heard about him before I had the privilege of knowing him...he was given the nickname "the Ogontz Preacher." Yes, he was that person who would always let you know what the Bible said concerning your filthy life and all of your dirty choices.

Let's remember where I was during this time. I loved my cultural experiences and my exposure to different lifestyles. I enjoyed the fact that I was embracing my Blackness and everything that entailed. I said nothing about church and relationship with God; that was very intentional. There was not one concern spent on God at this point; I kept him tucked deeply and very tight near my heart.

I even ended up joining the Black Students' Union! I was fully submerged. LOL! I was "woke." But in a real type of moment, I was blown away by the president's passion for his people and culture. He was a great inspiration and leader. He even allowed me to have a small leadership role too. He was genuinely committed to justice and equality. I'm sure he's still making a mark in the world.

Now back to the Ogontz Preacher, aka Rob, another giant in my life. I only have a handful, but he is most definitely in the number. He incited me internally, for that entire year. He knew the word of the Lord, and I didn't want to be that challenged. I still had the community choir I was in trying to make me honor my heart change and follow Christ since we ministered to folks who needed a genuine spirit.

I had Dr. Harvell consistently being her beautiful self, and I had Jose, who just exuded love. Now I had Rob telling folks to get their lives right before it was too late. He was such an inspiration. Yes, I was inspired yet again. I promise you need to have good examples to emulate—ones who will encourage you to be your best you on your worst days.

I sent Rob a thank you message some years ago because his voice stuck with me even when I left Ogontz to head to University Park, Penn State's main campus. And every now and I then I still hear him. My sophomore year required me to buckle down not only spiritually, but academically as well. I tried my absolute best, I promise you I did, but I still ended up not passing one of my prereqs for my major and PSU said I could come to U. Park, but I WILL be retaking this course. LOL! It was hard in those collegiate streets.

Rob, thank you for being light in what could've been an even darker time. I also had a great counselor, who was down to earth and just a straight shooter. She kept me on track with my academics and always had a pleasant word to say, no matter how her day was going. They were my "angels" and were present when I needed them most. My second year as a wild college student was now in the books, and it was time to hit the road to University Park.

Before we dive in, let me include a few fun facts:

1. Husband also started his college career at the Ogontz Campus in 1995 and was at University Park awaiting my arrival and, no, I did NOT go to Penn State because he did...judge someone else.
2. My Big Sissy Aronissa attended PSU as well, but she was a genius and started at University Park in 1995 also (...show off!)
3. Most of my Ogontz family also came to University Park with me. They were supposed to be keeping me grounded. They were supposed to remind me that being reckless didn't look good on me since I had that down already. SMH. LOL! All truths.

We are now at the beginning of my life's greatest moments. Lady had me all packed, and we were off to State College. I chose to live off campus. I had no Harvell, no Jose, no preaching Rob. None of those folks were in my immediate sight. Lord, help me! My junior year didn't come without trials either. I had to face, head-on, the results of my former sins and went through times where I often said, "Man I should've just...," but I was in the thick of adulthood now. There was no turning back the hands of time.

Lady, who was and still is such an awesome mom, could only guide me from afar now. She was also gracious enough to send half of the rent money each month because I only worked part-time. I thank God she was so far away, though. It allowed me to go through the press. My junior, senior, and half of my additional senior years were about becoming the woman God was trying to make me see back in high school. I mean, most of my junior year, I was still "semi-saved." If we had a lot more time, we'd be able to dissect my triflingness, but this is a book written to uplift you. LOL!

I was in no position to be judgmental, and I learned that early in life. My junior year was the party year. I actually think that I was drinking more than studying, but I'm not sure, you know? The years 1999 to 2000 came and went so quickly that I almost forgot how God tried to slip the gospel choir in my life. Although I wasn't a member when I first learned about the choir via Husband and Niss-Biss, United Soul Ensemble U.S.E. was my "fun" place to praise God. I mean, I could sing, so why not?

Aronissa was directing the choir when I used to make my weekend trips to see my other Girls' high friends and Husband, before me becoming a main campus student. She would always make me sing. Since I was living there now, joining was easy. I knew a few upper-classmen and women from the choir. It was cool because they looked out for me when I first got there, and I'd also see them at "the Robe" (PSU old-school insider).

Unfortunately, NissBiss and I didn't get to spend as much time together as I had planned. Eventually, she moved back to Philly to continue growing and being her awesome self. It was good to know she wasn't that far away. Having her close helped me realize that I wasn't completely devoid of human decency and morals. When God calls you, it's kind of hard to run forever. I didn't want to see how long forever was, so I'd support Husband and my friends by sitting in on a few U.S.E. rehearsals since he was one of the drummers.

My friend and I would mostly come to rehearsals, sit in the back, laugh, eat, and act like fools. Yeah, I think that's how I recall the whole Fall semester of 1999. LOL! I would then share all of my "wisdom" with the choir leadership so that they could make it better. I was just your average jerk. Yep...that was me. I want to say thanks to the fellas who were in charge, too, they never smote me. The director, who was always so wise, said, "Why don't you just join next semester and help direct?"

HAAAAAAAHAAAAAAA! Did you hear that laugh? He didn't realize that these college students probably didn't want to learn from the person who was constantly talking and laughing during their rehearsals. But that's when it began. God was trying to get my attention again. In my spring semester, I officially joined the almighty United Soul Ensemble, go U.S.E.!

I was an alto and also subbed in as one of the choir directors. This new assignment came with a shift, a level of awareness in my personal life. I didn't get everything in order immediately, but I recognized that change was imminent and required of me. I was no longer just a member/leader of the local church praise and worship team. I was no longer just the party animal who judged from the back of a classroom. I was no longer just an Accounting student. I was now stepping into the woman we see today.

I had to decide if I'd be a believer who would lead or a believer who would just follow. And don't trip, every good leader knows how to follow first. God, in His infinite wisdom, sent a young woman who was on all the fire in the world about Jesus. Not void of being housed in a tent of flesh, but a vocal lover of the Lord.

Her name is thee Mrs. Michelle Early (previously Massie). She married the bro Big Miiiiiiiiiike, and they trusted Husband and me to be their first daughter's godparents. Much love and hugz to my Kadence, aka KNEes. And another big one goes to our other niece Anaya, my twin. Michelle loved me so much that her second daughter was born on my birthday. Now back to the history lesson.

She met Husband before I started going to PSU Main, so I was looking forward to meeting her. Her reputation preceded her, and every person who knew her echoed the same sentiments. So when I set foot on PSU's main campus in the fall of 1999, I made it one of my top priorities to find her. She and I would become close friends in the spring the semester of 2000. The best decision God presented to me ever.

Initially, she wasn't that forceful about what I "needed" to do, but all of that niceness changed when we found out that she was assuming the role of president of the choir. She made it clear to me, in so many words, that she was happy to see me directing, but in the fall of 2000, I was going to be the only director. In addition to that, she let me know that I needed to ensure that my life was an open and living example. She also mentioned something about God calling me and me having to step into my next and yadda yadda yadda. Boy, am I glad that I met you, Shellz!

I just want to say that I thank you for your long speeches after a 2-hour rehearsal. The mini-sermons you'd preach to us, as if we were the only sinners in the world, are unforgettable. The correction you'd give was harsh at times, but necessary. The ability you had to show me your weaknesses in your strength, and the way you opened up your heart was unmatched.

You left your mind unlocked when I'd doubt myself. And the time, which you ain't never gettin' back, was well spent. Most importantly, I thank you for your love because it allowed you to give and do everything I could summarize and so much more. You have been and are a consistent voice in my life, and if you had not challenged my "norm," I would not have been so willing to be so unapologetically me.

Thank God for you and your family welcoming the SessomsFam into all of their homes and hearts as well. I wasn't always proud of me, but you were there to pick me up and give me a swift kick in the behind to keep me moving. I mean, you were my maid of honor/videographer for goodness sake. And a quick shout out to our best man, who hummed the Ginuwine song "Pony" as we exited the courthouse...so yeah, that's our wedding song now—a total mess. LOL! We rock out whenever we hear it.

I know I skipped the part about getting married while still in college, but here's the story in a nutshell. Juan and I had been together for seven years and wanted to make this thing officially official. We realized that we couldn't shack because we were leaders in every way imaginable, and to be effective, that would require us not to taint our witness. We were in love and knew this was our ultimate step. So, without compulsion or the aid of alcohol, we decided to get married on September 1, 2000. It was the best decision I could ever make.

So there we were, college students who, in my opinion, were responsible for one of the most amazing runs of U.S.E.; I was directing (and being mean, I heard). I loved all of my band members, and they were such an eclectic group of musicians. We had some of the most trainable voices who didn't always like me, but knew I was just trying to pull out their inner greatness. I am grateful to all of you! Much love to you all!

U.S.E. was my outlet, my safe place, and I was doing what my big sister, Aronissa, had done years prior. Isn't that interesting how I walked in her footsteps almost to a tee? I got married first, but other than that, we were twins, LHTG (insider). Some of those U.S.E. members even joined our group, 1Prayz Ministries. I hear they have a single out entitled "My Joy," and it's being sold on iTunes right now! My husband teamed up with his best friend to create Drum.Key Productions and the rest was history. These times marked the beginning stages of our musical callings. All of the individuals who played a role in the group, in 2002, are the real MVPs.

My life, however, wasn't just going to choir rehearsals. Husband and I made State College our home. We formed relationships that are still solid today. Let's discuss this training ground, where I learned more about Jesus and all things concerning Him. I attended a local church, Unity Church of Jesus Christ (UCJC), occasionally, and as I matured in my relationship with the Lord, I found so many jewels there.

There was this constant longing for more, but Husband and I were still opposed to the idea that we'd become residents of State College for seriousness, I mean we were Philadelphians. We were supposed to be in and out. When we finally joined UCJC, some five years later, after coming regularly, everyone asked us if we were sure we hadn't become members years ago. Funny, but where do I begin? Let me start by saying thank you to Pastors Harold and Sherren McKenzie for being authentic. We were able to step into ministry leadership for the first time under their guidance.

I grew in the prophetic and submitted to Unity's great leadership that aided in me becoming a great follower of Christ first and everything else second. Each member of the leadership team was impactful in my life as well as that of my family. Those who willingly volunteer to serve in a ministry so transient and offer up their entire lives as examples are nothing short of mind-blowing. What a blessing!

While I should NOT begin to name names, I have to say thank you to Uncle Wayne for being an excellent leader in praise and worship. I was able to develop my skills with you and recognize the anointing when I saw and felt it. Your jokes and approach to leadership was so refreshing. You were knowledgeable and just a lover of God.

I would also like to thank Aunt Beckye (Uncle Willie), Aunt Chris (Uncle Larry), and Aunt Barbara (Uncle Edgar). These three couples not only treated us like their children, but they were like my family. I can vividly recall moments at their houses when I'd download real-time wisdom and not that shady type either...it was that transparent kind. I submitted to their leadership in and outside of the church. 1 Peter 5:5 says, "Likewise, you who are younger, be subject to the elders."

My favorite time was the year I decided to wear jeans, t-shirts, and sneaks to church. These three classy women kindly pulled me aside and gave me a good ole-fashioned beat down. Just know that was the absolute last day I came in like that. It matters how you look and portray yourself, indeed. These women are examples in their walk with God, their marriages, their parenting skills, their professions, and so much more. I am so blessed to have them in my life.

To this day, if I call and ask for advice, they are there, even when I'm not a fan of their suggestions. LOL! I am grateful for the Garoians, the Abdullahs, the Rannies, the DavisFam, Aunt Roberta, Aunt Vicky, the Hayes', and every family or individual who prayed and spoke life into us over the 11 years we lived in State College. Aunt Di...your visions were right, and I love you so much for seeing beyond what I often preferred to present to others. Your laugh is forever in my heart.

I had to take that moment, readers. You must go back to a time where you had no clue what your life would end up looking like to remember that God had you the whole time. He's smart that way. He kept real-life examples in front of me consistently, and then He gave me TLynn (Terri Parker formerly Dowdy). Before she got married, she and I became close friends after Aronissa invited me into her circle of friends.

After getting married to the big bro, Curtis, we all became tighter than tight, and they even blessed Husband and me by asking us to be their daughter's godparents...hey Morgan Puddin' Pie! We were honored and shocked that they didn't let our parenting techniques scare them. What? We only beat our kids some, okay, ALL of the time. LOL! Spare the rod...you know the rest. Through my college years, and after graduation, TLynn became my living conscience.

She was the one human on earth that echoed what I knew was right. When I thought I'd be alone because my close friends had returned home after we graduated and there'd be no one left to calm my "crazy," God gave Terri all the tools in her tool shed to talk me off many a bridge. She and I developed a bond that is still very much alive even though we don't talk to one another daily. You have to know that God exists when He creates beings as humble and loving as she is.

I'm sure I have said it before, but if not, you get mad props for keeping my thoughts and sometimes actions from going from the ground floor straight to the penthouse suite. I had a tendency, in my period of growing, to go from zero to a million. I am just thankful for TLynn, and all of those I met along the way that helped me see Jesus in every situation I encountered. I know you all enjoyed going down memory lane with me, that was great for me too.

When people ask me how I have so much faith today, I can't forsake my past and all the beautiful people who directed me to my Daddy's arms, where I am always safe. State College was the place where I found hope in God. My training ground and my formative years in college produced hope. It was strengthened the most during that time.

Hope is a feeling of expectation and desire for a certain thing to happen; a feeling of trust. My question is simple: What or who do you have hope in? I can name a few people off the top of my mind, but you must know that hope in anyone other than God will leave you feeling pain, hurt, regret, disappointment, et cetera. Now faith is the assurance of things hoped for, the conviction of things not seen, according to verse 1 of Hebrews chapter 11.

Let's continue reading. Verses two and three say,

"²For by it the people of old received their commendation. ³By faith we understand that the universe was created by the word of God, so that what is seen was not made out of things that are visible."

Pause. Wait a minute. Is Hebrews 11:1 NOT the definition of faith? I'm not a professional, but I would say that we need to read the Bible in proper context.

If we take into account verses two and three, we notice that Paul continues in his explanation of what faith is and begins to reference people of the Old Testament. He explains how they had faith but didn't receive what God ultimately had promised. The book of Hebrews is such a meaty book of the Bible. Promise me that you will read it, okay? Don't stop at chapter 11. Keep going. We have a choice. We either believe in evolution or believe that God created the world and everything in it by speaking things into existence.

I'm sure you can say that there are more options, but this book is about faith. We will stick with those two. I believe the latter, which allows verse one to make a lot more sense. Hebrews 11 begins to give examples of those in the Old Testament who exhibited a measure of faith. They had to believe in a God they could not see, for an outcome they hoped would be beneficial for them.

Believing in God and seeing Him move on their behalf was their evidence that God was, indeed, real. Verse two simply points out that we are not going to receive a reward for having faith, but we will please the Lord, which is the greatest commendation of every commendation. Get it? What I'm saying is simple. We are in this world to live by faith, since without it, we cannot please God (Hebrews 11:6), to gain a simple smile from God.

At times those smiles and warm fuzzies from our Heavenly Father come with a hefty price in the world. I'm certain Noah was not feeling his best when ridiculed for building the ark. Moses, as described in Hebrews, was looking for a reward, yes, not for things, but for seeing God. Our time, the time after Jesus, is a little different. We have a goal in mind, an eternal reward. What prize is better than Heaven?

I had hope as I evolved. I hoped that God had better for me, that if I was His workmanship, created in Christ Jesus for good works, which He prepared beforehand, that I should walk in them (Eph. 2:10 paraphrased). I hoped my life would get better as I gave myself entirely to Him. I had hope, even if I wasn't invited to a party or was left out because I was always in church somewhere. I had hope that my consistency would be pleasing to the Lord.

I had hope that Jesus interceded for me, even at my lowest points, some I am too embarrassed and ashamed to even utter. My college years, flaws and all, with many more mistakes and poor judgment calls ahead of me, kept me hopeful. I had hope in who I could not see because Jesus gave His life for me. God loved the world so much that He sent His only son for my past, current, and future sins.

Now, I have hope and confidence in the Lord because I believe that I will someday meet Him in the air. So, what's faith got to do with it?

— ·· — ·· — ·

Your Lifework:

Do me a favor, will you? Study these scriptures which I'm writing in no particular order of importance since the entire Bible is full of wisdom:

- Psalm 147:11
- Proverbs 10:28
- Isaiah 40:31
- Philippians 1:6
- Romans 5:2-7; 8:24-28; 15:13

Use your prayer and journaling time to consider, truthfully, where your hope lies.

Is it your job, the one God gave you? Is it your spouse, the man or woman God sent to you? Is it your wealth, the money God gifted you? Is it your friends, the ones God gave you? You get it? Do you have misdirected hope? Do you put your hope in things and people? This is a judgment-free zone in real life.

I desire to see your lifework become your life's work. A life that truly pleases God. Yes, YOU CAN please the Father. We have the best intercession partner ever, Jesus Himself. And let's not forget that Holy Spirit indwells us and intercedes on our behalf too.

This fight is FIXED...we always win! Place your hope in God... the best choice you will ever make. I heard that the prize is worth it!

6

What's Faith Got To Do With It?

*Now to him who is able to do far more abundantly
than all that we ask or think, according to the power
at work within us, to him be glory in the church and
in Christ Jesus throughout all generations, forever
and ever. Amen.*
Eph. 3:20-21

" STAND KNOWING THAT FERVOR, ATTENTION, INTIMACY, TENACITY, "
AND HOPE ARE NOT ONLY POSSIBLE BUT NECESSARY. THEY COME
WITH A PROMISE. SO LIVE YOUR LIFE AS A FAITH STALKER. DON'T
THINK, JUST LEAP!

Here's the thing...I'm no expert on faith, no expert on the Bible,
no expert in relationships, no real expert in most situations. Still, I
know this, I became an expert in learning. See, when you position
yourself to learn always, you become an expert student. The Bible
says that we should do our best to present ourselves to God as one
approved, a worker who does not need to be ashamed, rightly han-
dling the word of truth (2 Timothy 2:15).

What does that mean? It merely means that we need to be ones
who love to study God's word, not just for the sake of studying,
but to be sure we can inform those who don't know the Lord inti-

mately. We should be in a posture where we have our ears against the heart of the Father. Yeah, that may seem rain puddle deep to some, but if you truly live a life focused on what the Lord says, your faith will grow stronger as you begin to see Him move on your behalf.

Your faith will grow stronger as you start to see Him move on behalf of those you've prayed for, those with whom you are close. He can handle the small battles as well as the gihugic wars that you find yourself fighting. Thus, we should live a life of daily repentance and adhere to the words of the gospel (Mark 1:15). The end game is what's at stake.

I've noticed that throughout my childhood, adolescent years, and now in adulthood, I have sometimes repented more than I gave thanks. While this book isn't a story about my entire life, it is about me entering a place where faith was the beginning and end for me, no matter what. I live so far on the edge of insanity now, more than I ever have. I was able to jump on this Texas bandwagon because Jesus sacrificed His life for me. He died on the cross for me to not only obey God, but to trust Him with all that I was and all I was going to become.

After all, Jesus is the founder and perfecter of my faith (Heb 12:2). Faith was the only thing I had. It's the only thing I HAVE. I frequently and regularly sinned, but God still allowed me to wake up with new mercies every day. My college experiences and the people I've met since then propelled me to seek out the God who loved me enough to give me a million and twenty chances. I had to come to grips with some hard truths about myself along the journey. I had to snap out of my world and admit I was lost. Legit lost.

I finally realized that I didn't truly trust God. This whole journey has been REAL in real life. You see, trust is a mandatory attribute for having faith as well. I've come to learn that <u>F</u>ervor, <u>A</u>ttention, <u>I</u>ntimacy, <u>T</u>enacity, and <u>H</u>ope are the ingredients of faith. Even when we look at notable characters in the Bible, we see that they possessed all of those traits, Jesus included.

These thoughts bring me to Ephesians 2 verses 4-10 where it reads:

> "*[4]But God, being rich in mercy, because of the great love with which he loved us, [5]even when we were dead in our trespasses, made us alive together with Christ—by grace you have been saved— [6]and raised us up with him and seated us with him in the heavenly places in Christ Jesus, [7]so that in the coming ages he might show the immeasurable riches of his grace in kindness toward us in Christ Jesus. [8]For by grace you have been saved through faith. And this is not your own doing; it is the gift of God, [9]not a result of works, so that no one may boast. [10]For we are his workmanship, created in Christ Jesus for good works, which God prepared beforehand, that we should walk in them.*"

Catch this! The life I was living wasn't even mine. Who was I to decide whether or not I'd go to seminary, move to Texas, or become a Pastor? Who was I? I was chosen, and not the other way around. God trusted me with the hearts and lives of the people He sent directly to me. I was supposed to show them Christ consistently. I was uberly unsuccessful most times, but quite honestly, I grew tired of not being obedient.

I found that 1 Samuel 15 was how I began to feel about my very own life. Verses 20-26 read as follows:

> *"²⁰And Saul said to Samuel, "I have obeyed the voice of the Lord. I have gone on the mission on which the Lord sent me. I have brought Agag the king of Amalek, and I have devoted the Amalekites to destruction. ²¹But the people took of the spoil, sheep and oxen, the best of the things devoted to destruction, to sacrifice to the Lord your God in Gilgal." ²²And Samuel said, "Has the Lord as great delight in burnt offerings and sacrifices, as in obeying the voice of the Lord? <u>Behold, to obey is better than sacrifice</u>, and to listen than the fat of rams. ²³For rebellion is as the sin of divination, and presumption is as iniquity and idolatry. Because you have rejected the word of the Lord, he has also rejected you from being king."²⁴Saul said to Samuel, "I have sinned, for I have transgressed the commandment of the Lord and your words, because I feared the people and obeyed their voice. ²⁵Now therefore, please pardon my sin and return with me that I may bow before the Lord." ²⁶And Samuel said to Saul, "I will not return with you. For you have rejected the word of the Lord, and the Lord has rejected you from being king over Israel."*

Too cold, too soon. I had to take a more extended look in the mirror and snap out of this whole, "I got it syndrome" and leave behind the whole "I have a Plan B, C, D, and HH if God doesn't come through on time." Trust me, you still have some time as long as you're inhaling and exhaling, praise be to God! The Old Testament was brutal. If God wasn't smiting folks, He was putting them on public blast.

Somebody say, "Thank you Lord for not putting my business on Front Street!" And let me drop this right here as well, God does

NOT operate on our time. Shame on you man and woman of God who prays to the Father with a timeline. You crack me up, telling Him how this happened the same time three years ago, and how it's been taking years since you've heard answers. He will, without saying one word, show you how to hurry up and wait.

Stop trying to impose your finite selves on our infinite God. STOP THAT! Do you want to be like the children of Israel in real life? Go ahead and tell God about your deadlines and your plans. Speaking of the Israelites, it took me almost 40 years, isn't that ironic, but I finally got it. Texas and this new life's journey is where He wanted it to be, right in HIS hands.

"Obedience is better than sacrifice" is a loaded statement because you need to sacrifice for obedience; just ask Abraham and Isaac. A friend of mine once asked me how I made the struggle look so easy. I had to pause at first but because I knew she was genuinely asking a question, my answer was what you have seen echoed throughout this text: Do you trust God or don't you? Yes, I answered a question with a question.

The struggle is par for the course. Jesus understood the struggle. The disciples, our models, were murdered and mistreated for the sake of His name. Who was I to live a life contrary to that? While my struggle looked like a cakewalk to others, I suffered silently. I had to grow to love myself. I had to learn to forgive myself. I had to master fighting through temptations of just being a jerk and not caring about what would come of my life.

I had to put on my big girl boots and face the facts. God chose me. He loved me enough to send His only son. My Lord knew who I would become before I was formed, and He also knew that I'd struggle. He knew it all. This leap of faith we took, ultimately as a family, was the solidifying directive for me. Moving to Texas meant leaving everything I knew that appeared to be reasonable and comfortable. I was ridding myself of the temptations of the world that would so easily entice me (Hebrews 12:1 paraphrased).

I was leaving the city where I grew up. Philly used to be my everything; I put my hope in my town. God put the move so deep in my mind and soul that I am not even thinking about ever moving back to my place of birth. I will always visit because we have family and friends there, but God put a new path in front of me, and this time I really trust Him. Our kids even made the most beautiful transition to this ole country state; God made our relocation seamless. My mother also migrated!

Even with the challenges we've faced here, we are determined to believe that this IS our land of milk and honey. I put my "all-in" faith where it finally belonged, in Jesus. I can do nothing with my power. Each day, hour, minute, and second all belong to the Master. The sooner we learn that, the better off we are. My journey may not be the same as yours, but we are all on one, nonetheless.

I like what 2 Timothy 2: 8-13 says:

> *"⁸Remember Jesus Christ, risen from the dead, the offspring of David, as preached in my gospel, ⁹for which I am suffering, bound with chains as a criminal. But the word of God is not bound! ¹⁰Therefore I endure everything for the sake of the elect, that they also may obtain the salvation that is in Christ Jesus with eternal glory. ¹¹The saying is trustworthy, for: If we have died with him, we*

will also live with him; [12]*if we endure, we will also reign with him;*
if we deny him, he also will deny us; [13]*if we are faithless, he re-*
mains faithful - for he cannot deny himself."

In the end, faith has everything to do with everything. Yes, I said
it right. Wherever God takes or leads me, is where I need to be. I can
go all over the world or continue ministering to the members we
have now at the Sound Of Worship Center. No matter what, it will
be worthwhile. Following His instructions, trusting and hoping in
Him, and believing His word is what I'm after. I don't get a treat or
a cookie from people for being an example of faith, but I do please
God. That's who matters the most.

Husband will tell you. Some days he'd look at me like, "Who
are you?" and "Are we seriously believing God at this level?" I live
on the edge of life, not knowing what is going to happen next because I have so much faith in God that if I'm doubting, I feel sick. In
real life. I MUST have faith. I have become a Faith Stalker, and I'm
proud of it.

I've changed my language, and if you don't hear faith when I talk,
I'm out of order. I encourage all of you to use this quick snapshot
of my faith journey to truly take the notion of "making sense" out
of your mind. Nothing about believing in God makes sense. For this
very reason, Christianity gets fought from every angle, and it will
continue to be until the end of time. Having faith and standing on
the word of God to support your faith may feel crazy, and it
may feel strange, but it is required of you.

I hear many people tell me that they'd never have the courage to
make such a bold move. I listen to them say that planting a church

in a foreign land with just four family members is insane. Folks say that they'd never write a book about their life, that they'd never this, never that, never, never, never. I got tired of hearing my old self in those I kept company with, so God kindly, and sometimes forcefully, removed them. Having faith is way bigger than what you could never do.

Duh! It's not about you. I vowed to be an example of God's love, mercy, grace, faithfulness, and all of those characteristics that we, as believers and followers of Christ, adore so much. Living each day as the needle on the compass is where I feel most comfortable. God controls the compass and points me where I need to be.

Darnell Jaxon wrote a song called "Perfect Security." It says, "Keep me in the shadow of your wings. For in you, I have perfect security. I'll forever love you and worship thee. For in you, I have perfect security. Keep me in the shadow of your wings. For in you, I have perfect security. I'll forever trust you and follow thee. For in you, I have perfect security...yeeeeeeaaaah." I can't wait until he releases that song to the masses. It's the ultimate state of living...knowing that in God's arms, you're safe. It doesn't even matter when trouble comes, because it will. What matters is where your faith lies.

So I ask you this...are you depending on yourself and your will? The will of the universe? The will of mother nature and all of her splendor? The will of the ancestors? The will of the scientists? Or are you genuinely co-dependent? I've told you who I was...you can call me Faith Stalker #1. Join me and insert your life, story, journey, marriage, children, job, friendships, and relationships, add all of that into these pages.

If you tried to do it alone, you still have time to let God reign. It's easier, it's less stressful, it's painful at times, but let me tell you, even in your pain, your loss, and sometimes your suffering, you rejoice in it. I don't even know how I do it. I just have this untamed, uncharacteristic type of faith. I'll leave you with this, James 2:14-26:

"14 What good is it, my brothers, if someone says he has faith but does not have works? Can that faith save him? 15 If a brother or sister is poorly clothed and lacking in daily food, 16 and one of you says to them, "Go in peace, be warmed and filled," without giving them the things needed for the body, what good is that? 17 So also faith by itself, if it does not have works, is dead. 18 But someone will say, "You have faith and I have works." Show me your faith apart from your works, and I will show you my faith by my works. 19 You believe that God is one; you do well. Even the demons believe—and shudder! 20 Do you want to be shown, you foolish person, that faith apart from works is useless? 21 Was not Abraham our Father justified by works when he offered up his son Isaac on the altar? 22 You see that faith was active along with his works, and faith was completed by his works; 23 and the Scripture was fulfilled that says, "Abraham believed God, and it was counted to him as righteousness"—and he was called a friend of God. 24 You see that a person is justified by works and not by faith alone. 25 And in the same way was not also Rahab the prostitute justified by works when she received the messengers and sent them out by another way? 26 For as the body apart from the spirit is dead, so also faith apart from works is dead."

Faith is not just doing; it's not just talking; it's all about living. You see shirts that say, "Worship is a lifestyle." I'm not in disagreement with that statement, but without faith, you don't even know how to worship correctly. You must speak the language of faith. It's the only currency that works in the spirit.

You have to possess a measure of faith in your daily interactions. From tithing to praying, you need to have FAITH. When I changed the way I talked, God showed me another side of Him. I longed for this side, but couldn't quite decipher what was tugging on me. My prayer is that you, too, become a Faith Stalker, keeping faith first... always.

— ·· — ·· — ·

Your Lifework:

So you've been given a snapshot of my life, my woes, and my challenges to obey the Lord. You've read about my journey, as a disciple of Christ, to walk by FAITH. You've watched me go from a part-time believer to a full-fledged Faith Stalking child of the King. You've seen God open doors for me that I thought would never come ajar because of the life I used to live. You've seen how the faith I now have has wholly taken over not just my life, but that of my family's because, daily, they go along with my new "crazy" way of living.

You've heard the words crazy, impossible, insanity, and you're probably like, uhhhhh, I'm not sure about any of those things for me. And that, my dear sisters and brothers, is the issue. You're not crazy enough. You're not on edge enough. You're not insane enough. You're not really sold out to the life you claim you live. If you were, you'd see more signs and wonders, see God make ways out of no way, experience the Holy Spirit's instructions like you never have, and live a life of freedom.

TRUE freedom in the King! Now my level of faith didn't happen overnight. You've had a front-row seat in my progression and how I recognized God working on my behalf, although sometimes it took a long time for me to get it. What my "crazy" looks like may not be the same for you, and that's okay. We are peculiar and created individually on purpose for a purpose. But please catch this.

You will not get to where God desires you to be without a RAD-ICAL measure of F.A.I.T.H....Fervor, Attentiveness, Intimacy, Tenacity, and Hope.

What I've realized in life is that I've been living on the "40 acres and a mule" kind of hopes and the "making sure my kids would be secure when I was gone" kind of dreams. God wants me to own many houses and thousands of acres of land, He wants me to have businesses all over the world, and He wants me to establish a legacy for my grandchildren's children's grandchildren. You and I both have placed limits on an infinite God. We all have fallen victim to that mistake, hence the reason why I wrote this book.

I hear people in my circle tell me how much this text is needed and how timely it is, and while I agree, I have to be transparent when I say, "Okay...and?" We have access to the most important and most timely book every single day. We don't delve into, follow, or seek answers from it, so why is this book any different? If we don't want to follow the Bible, how can someone's faith be jump started from this book? And God said to me as plainly as He always does, "It will work because I said it would." I love answers like that. And I have to trust and believe that the Lord knows way more than I do and that these words are necessary.

It only takes one person to make a change in your life, in the world, and prayerfully I am that one for you. Your Lifework is not only challenging, but it will be unsettling. It's not a formula you haven't heard before. However, faith is something you've struggled with because the world is still getting worse. The Church still has its deep woes. We don't see deliverance happening as it should. Leadership is out of order. Suicide in the Kingdom is increasing at alarming rates, and the world still feels like they can trample on believers. Do I need to go on?

Faith is lost, faith is lacking, faith is sometimes non-existent, and NOW is the time to use that defibrillator and say, "CLEAR!" Yes, restart your commitment to the Father. Repent and ask the Lord to give you fresh eyes to see what's ahead. Ask for Jesus to intercede on your behalf like never before, because THIS time, you are ready to be who you were designed and created to be. Ask Holy Spirit to indwell and guide you like never before, because THIS time is different.

THIS time you want more than favor, and you're coming for everything the enemy stole and tried to take. You want DOUBLE for your trouble. THIS time your FAITH will be beyond 100%. With this new faith stalking life, you will live unashamed. You'll be on fire and excited to tell every man, woman, girl, and boy about the God you serve. You'll be telling everyone about the miracles He's performing in your life and the lives of everyone connected to you.

You have an official restart button, so go ahead, click it, and begin your new Lifework! God has not created you to live in fear of what's next, of what you will eat or wear, in fear of even failing. When you fail, take it as an opportunity to learn and grow. It is NOT the end of your journey. Failing feels horrible, yes. I'm going on and on because I sincerely believe that as our faith builds as a body, we will be able to make a significant difference in our world.

It's incredible when believers come together in faith, from all parts of the world, in all fields of expertise and desire to be better disciples. Our children will be watching us change the world and will learn what it means to pick up your cross and follow Christ. FAITH is trusting that God's plans are higher than yours could ever be. FAITH is knowing that suffering and failure may come, but not for naught. FAITH is putting on your seat belts and getting strapped in for the best ride of your life. FAITH is MANDATORY. FAITH is MANDATORY. FAITH is MANDATORY. And get this, it's not something we should have when it's convenient for us.

You should wake up with your FAITH STALKER mindset every single day. You shouldn't leave home without your tools. So I said all of that to say, your FAITHstart (aka Fresh Start) opportunity has arrived. Don't sulk over why things didn't work in the past. Don't harbor ill-will or think about all you missed out on, don't do that. Do this:

- Repent (2 Chronicles 7:14; Joel 2:13; 2 Peter 3:9)
- Regroup (Isaiah 40:30-31)
- Restart (Job 8:7; 2 Corinthians 5:17)
- FAITH STALK (Isaiah 43:18-19; Philippians 3:13-14)

And know this, God can use whomever He chooses to use, but the blessing comes when you know He wants to use YOU. Don't miss this movement. Don't miss this life-changing event. Don't miss out on helping someone who has no idea they need what's inside of you. When I was in sales, they would encourage us to travel to the "big" events. In that type of environment, you'd see the victories, losses, and overcoming testimonies of others that would always propel you. It would almost force you to dig deeper than you ever had before to achieve higher heights. So imagine that this is a big event!

You've spent your money to hear about my losses, trials, and overcoming testimonies during the essential part of my walk, my faith journey. You've related to the times in your life when you knew you could do more and be more, but you fell on hard times and unbelief, worry, and doubt set in. You know NOW that THIS time is DIFFERENT. Your next days WILL be better than your previous days. Your losses will seem small because your eyes will remain on the ultimate prize, and THIS time, your FAITH will not waiver. You will begin to walk out Deuteronomy 28, and you will bring others to the God you serve because of the FAITHStalking life you live.

Fervor, Attention, Intimacy, Tenacity, and Hope are the ingredients of FAITH.

That's what this life we are living is all about. And before we leave, I want to pray...

I pray that You, the Creator of the world, the God who knows all, sees all, the ever-loving, ever-caring, ever-merciful, ever-faithful God, the author and finisher of my faith, Jesus, who is my favorite big brother that died just for me and intercedes on my behalf, and Holy Spirit who indwells us, all who desire to be filled, to seal these words. I ask that you touch these hearts and households. I ask that you honor their first steps toward FAITH Stalking. Cover and strengthen, God. Amen.

TODAY is YOUR DAY!!! #TeamFaithStalking on the rise. You got this! I'm praying with and for you. Your journey is NOT over!

Welcome to my world!

Faith Stalking 101 has commenced

Remember...you gotta have FAITH!

#FaithFirst

Catch the movement!

Faith Stalker University

CONGRATULATIONS!!! You made it! You've passed your first class in the newly built Faith Stalker University. Faith Stalking means to stealthily take one blind step at a time. Therefore, a Faith Stalker is a *person* who stealthily takes one blind step at a time. WELCOME!!! Print your name on your certificate, date it, take a picture of it, and upload it to every social media outlet with the hashtags: #HIFIO, #FaithStalking101, #HowIFaithedItOver, #FaithFirst, and #FaithStalker.

Don't forget to keep your **Fervor,** remember to pay **Attention**, focus on your **Intimacy** with God, keep a **Tenacious** spirit about you, and never lose **Hope** in the only true and wise God. I look forward to meeting you someday at a conference or book signing or virtual book tour, and don't forget to grab your workbook coming out soon as well. We are in this Faith Stalk together.

Stay Blessed,

Sonya M. Sessoms, MBA, MDiv.

Certificate

Certificate of Completion

THIS DOCUMENT CERTIFIES THAT

HAS SUCCESSFULLY COMPLETED THE

FAITH STALKER 101

TRAINING COURSE

DATE

FAITH STALKER #1

"How I Faithed It Over" Challenge

Now it's your turn to hit the reset button! You have your certificate of completion in hand, and your life is depending on your next move. You also have to remember that your next steps will help the lives of those you still haven't met. So choose FAITH!!! I'm just saying, don't waste any more time. Be on the lookout for a jump start to 2021 with my 30-Day "How I Faithed it Over" Challenge!

You will receive the upcoming workbook for a discounted price if you send a screenshot of your receipt of this book's purchase (ebooks included) to the email below on or before October 2, 2020: 30DayChallenge@howifaitheditover.com.

Once I hear from you, and as soon as the workbook is ready for sale, I will notify you FIRST so that you can pre-order it with your discount before it hits the general public. To show you how honored I am that you want to continue your faith journey with me, I'll send you a PDF file of the first chapter of the workbook (once my publisher says I can). I want to ensure you are focused and ready to Faith Stalk like never before.

I'm so pumped about us embarking on this Faith Stalking way of life. It will prove to be a blessing to you and all those you encounter. No matter what life brings to your doorstep, ask God how to get you to what He has next. He will allow Holy Spirit to speak to you so that change and victory will be your forever story.

There's nothing like having friends on the journey with you. Follow us on all social media outlets and get ready for our peer groups on Facebook. We need to encourage one another. We want to have space dedicated for all of our Faith Stalkers to testify, get prayer, and drop those praise reports. And don't forget to bring your children along for the movement, you're never too young.

See you soon, fellow Faith Stalker!

Photographer: Tanisha Dunham of LightLens Photography
Makeup: Sherri Robinson of Visions in Beauty
Hair: Jamez Smith of Hairtique Color & Design

Pastor Sonya M. Sessoms, affectionately known as "Pastor Sone," is a wife, mother, serial entrepreneur, and lyricist. She is an all-in Jesus follower who looks for opportunities to share her love for Christ and to fulfill the role of a faith-filled believer. She is known for speaking the truth in love without holding back. She passionately believes that walking in faith is "not hocus-pocus, not 'name it and claim it,' but being obedient to the voice of the Holy Spirit."

How I Faithed It Over is her first published work and was birthed from her passion for God and her love of people. Born and raised in Philadelphia, PA, Pastor Sone maintains a strong connection to her hometown and credits her time at her alma mater, the

Philadelphia High School for Girls and Class 241, for helping her begin the journey of self-discovery. Pastor Sone is an alum of Penn State University (B.S., Accounting), Regis University (MBA, Finance and Accounting), and Biblical Theological Seminary (now Missio Seminary) where she earned a Master of Divinity degree. When asked what she does for a living, she often replies with, "I'm a Jackie of all trades."

She started her accounting company and very first business, SMS Works, as a student at Penn State in 2002. In that same year, she and her husband Juan "Darnell Jaxon" Sessoms founded 1Prayz Ministries. They are both accomplished singers, songwriters, and producers. 1Prayz's single, "My Joy," opened the door for them to let the world in on their passion and love for music, and they have more projects on the way.

*Photographer: Tanisha Dunham of
LightLens Photography*

CPSIA information can be obtained
at www.ICGtesting.com
Printed in the USA
LVHW110850140820
663150LV00002BA/143